3B

Math in Focus®
Singapore Math
by Marshall Cavendish

Extra Practice

Author
Bernice Lau Pui Wah

Marshall Cavendish
Education

US Distributor

HOUGHTON MIFFLIN HARCOURT

COMMON CORE

© Copyright 2009, 2013 Edition Marshall Cavendish International (Singapore) Private Limited

Published by Marshall Cavendish Education
An imprint of Marshall Cavendish International (Singapore) Private Limited
Times Centre, 1 New Industrial Road, Singapore 536196
Customer Service Hotline: (65) 6411 0820
E-mail: tmesales@sg.marshallcavendish.com
Website: www.marshallcavendish.com/education

Distributed by
Houghton Mifflin Harcourt
222 Berkeley Street
Boston, MA 02116
Tel: 617-351-5000
Website: www.hmheducation.com/mathinfocus

First published 2009
2013 Edition

Math in Focus® Extra Practice 3B
ISBN 978-0-669-01566-9

Printed in Singapore

2 3 4 5 6 7 8   1401   18 17 16 15 14 13
4500404079   A B C D E

Contents

CHAPTER 16
Time and Temperature

CHAPTER 17
Angles and Lines

CHAPTER 18
Two-Dimensional Shapes

CHAPTER 19

Area and Perimeter

Introducing

Math in Focus®

Extra Practice

Extra Practice 3A and *3B*, written to complement *Math in Focus®: Singapore Math by Marshall Cavendish* Grade 3, offer further practice very similar to the Practice exercises in the Student Books and Workbooks for on-level students.

Extra Practice provides ample questions to reinforce all the concepts taught, and includes challenging questions in the Put on Your Thinking Cap! pages. These pages provide extra non-routine problem-solving opportunities, strengthening critical thinking skills.

Extra Practice is an excellent option for homework, or may be used in class or after school. It is intended for students who simply need more practice to become confident, or secure students who are aiming for excellence.

BLANK

CHAPTER 10 Money

Lesson 10.1 Addition

Find each missing amount.

1. $12.25 + $26.55 = $_____

$12 25¢ $26 55¢

$12 + $26 = $_____

25¢ + 55¢ = _____¢

$_____ + _____¢ = $_____

2. $24.05 + $35.75 = $_____

$24 5¢ $35 75¢

$_____ + $_____ = $_____

_____¢ + _____¢ = _____¢

$_____ + _____¢ = $_____

Add.

3. $12.85 + $18.00 = $_____

4. $2.45 + $0.35 = $_____

5. $14.35 + $33.50 = $_____

6. $15.80 + $0.20 = $_____

7. $26.75 + $52.25 = $_____

8. $9.45 + $0.85 = $_____

9. $73.50 + $5.90 = $_____

Name: _____ **Date:** _____

Complete each number bond. Then add.

10. $17.35 + $0.80 = ?

$17.35 + $1 = $_____

$_____ − _____¢ = $_____

So, $17.35 + $0.80 = $_____

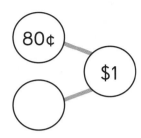

11. $26.70 + $0.85 = ?

$26.70 + $1 = $_____

$_____ − _____¢ = $_____

So, $26.70 + $0.85 = $_____

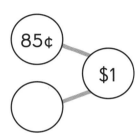

12. $34.45 + $0.75 = ?

$34.45 + $1 = $_____

$_____ − _____¢ = $_____

So, $34.45 + $0.75 = $_____

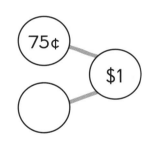

13. $48.50 + $0.90 = ?

$48.50 + $1 = $_____

$_____ − _____¢ = $_____

So, $48.50 + $0.90 = $_____

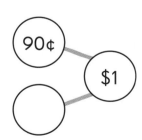

Add.

14. $3.20
       + $4.75
       _____
       $

15. $4.65
       + $5.33
       _____
       $

16. $ 9.70
       + $60.25
       _____
       $

17. $16.25
       + $ 3.50
       _____
       $

18. $33.35
       + $ 6.35
       _____
       $

19. $52.15
       + $ 4.85
       _____
       $

20. $85.95
       + $ 4.40
       _____
       $

21. $28.65
       + $21.85
       _____
       $

Name: _____   **Date:** _____

Look at the advertisement.

ITEMS ON SALE

art bag $15.55   lunch box $4.35   pencil case $3.90   school bag $29.50

book $0.80   water bottle $6.75   pen $1.65   drawing paper $2.50

Find each cost.

22. a lunch box and a water bottle	**23.** an art bag and a pencil case
24. two pens and a water bottle	**25.** a drawing paper and two school bags

Lesson 10.2   Subtraction

Find each missing amount.

1. $15.85 − $9.30 = $_____

$15   85¢ $9   30¢

$15 − $9 = $_____

85¢ − 30¢ = _____¢

$_____ + _____¢ = $_____

2. $48.65 − $24.45 = $_____

$48   65¢ $24   45¢

$_____ − $_____ = $_____

_____¢ − _____¢ = _____¢

$_____ + _____¢ = $_____

3. $66.80 − $45.30 = $_____

$66   80¢ $45   30¢

$_____ − $_____ = $_____

_____¢ − _____¢ = _____¢

$_____ + _____¢ = $_____

Subtract.

4. $8.65 − $4.00 = $_____

5. $28.85 − $0.45 = $_____

6. $55.90 − $24.20 = $_____

7. $9.70 − $0.65 = $_____

8. $69.80 − $7.10 = $_____

Complete the number bond. Then subtract.

9. $12.30 − $0.85 = ?

$12.30 − $1 = $_____

$_____ + _____¢ = $_____

So, $12.30 − $0.85 = $_____

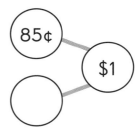

10. $20.50 − $0.95 = ?

$20.50 − $1 = $_____

$_____ + _____¢ = $_____

So, $20.50 − $0.95 = $_____

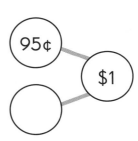

11. $15.20 − $1.90 = ?

$15.20 − $2 = $_____

$_____ + _____¢ = $_____

So, $15.20 − $1.90 = $_____

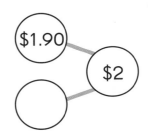

12. $18.40 − $2.80 = ?

$18.40 − $3 = $_____

$_____ + _____¢ = $_____

So, $18.40 − $2.80 = $_____

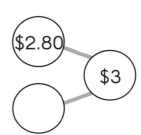

Subtract.

13.
$$\begin{array}{r} \$\,4.88 \\ -\ \$\,3.25 \\ \hline \$ \end{array}$$

14.
$$\begin{array}{r} \$\,9.76 \\ -\ \$\,6.20 \\ \hline \$ \end{array}$$

15.
$$\begin{array}{r} \$\,37.65 \\ -\ \$\,13.03 \\ \hline \$ \end{array}$$

16.
$$\begin{array}{r} \$\,48.80 \\ -\ \$\,23.50 \\ \hline \$ \end{array}$$

17.
$$\begin{array}{r} \$\,16.60 \\ -\ \$\ \ 2.54 \\ \hline \$ \end{array}$$

19.
$$\begin{array}{r} \$\,36.78 \\ -\ \$\,14.95 \\ \hline \$ \end{array}$$

19.
$$\begin{array}{r} \$\,85.05 \\ -\ \$\,21.60 \\ \hline \$ \end{array}$$

20.
$$\begin{array}{r} \$\,70.00 \\ -\ \$\,28.20 \\ \hline \$ \end{array}$$

Name: _____ Date: _____

How much change will Jansen receive? Complete the table.

	Amount Jansen had	Item bought	Change Received
21.		 $4.95	$ 1 0 . 0 0 − $ 4 . 9 5 ————— $
22.		$12.45	
23.		$19.80	
24.		 $39.90	

Lesson 10.3   Real-World Problems: Money

Solve. Draw bar models to help you.

1.   Mathew pays $52 for a pair of glasses.
    Raja pays $7.15 more for a different pair of glasses.
    How much does Raja pay for his pair of glasses?

2.   Mr. Larry buys a tennis racket for $76.90.
    He gives the cashier 2 fifty-dollar bills.
    How much change does Mr. Larry receive?

3.   Emily saves $28.60.
        Emily's sister saves $19.80 more than that.

      a.   How much money does Emily's sister save?
      b.   How much money do they save in all?

4.   Lily has $17.50.
        Zachary has $24.90.
        They want to buy a $60 present for their mother.

      a.   How much money do they have in all?
      b.   How much more money must they save if they want to buy the present?

 Put on Your Thinking Cap!

Draw the least number of bills and coins to make each amount.

Example

$12.45

| $10 | | $1 | | $1 |

(25¢) (10¢) (10¢)

1. $36.70

2. $57.35

Solve.

3.   Xavier has $12 less than Calvin.
Amelia has $18 more than Xavier.
They have a total of $102 altogether.
How much money does Xavier have?

4.   There are 20 coins in a piggy bank.
There are only dimes and quarters in the bank.
The total amount of money in the bank is $3.80.
How many quarters are in the piggy bank?

 CHAPTER 11

Metric Length, Mass, and Volume

Lesson 11.1   Meters and Centimeters

Write in centimeters.

1.   6 m 80 cm = _____ cm

2.   5 m 43 cm = _____ cm

3.   8 m 6 cm = _____ cm

4.   12 m 35 cm = _____ cm

5.   15 m 7 cm = _____ cm

6.   28 m 12 cm = _____ cm

1 m = 100 cm

Write in meters and centimeters.

7.   185 cm = _____ m _____ cm

8.   312 cm = _____ m _____ cm

9.   708 cm = _____ m _____ cm

10.   936 cm = _____ m _____ cm

11.   1,203 cm = _____ m _____ cm

Read the description. Write the name and height of each student. Then fill in the blanks.

12.

Mary: 1 meter 52 centimeters

Lucy: 137 centimeters

Eric: 143 centimeters

Ken: 1 meter 60 centimeters

Lucy _____   _____   _____

137 cm _____ cm   _____ cm   _____ cm

13. _____ is the tallest.

14. _____ is the shortest.

15. Mary is _____ centimeters taller than Eric.

Lesson 11. 2   Kilometers and Meters

Write in meters.

1.   8 km = _____ m

2.   4 km 350 m = _____ m

3.   7 km 900 m = _____ m

4.   5 km 10 m = _____ m

5.   2 km 95 m = _____ m

6.   7 km 9 m = _____ m

7.   3 km 5 m = _____ m

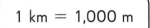

Write in kilometers and meters.

8.   5,000 m = _____ km

9.   6,340 m = _____ km _____ m

10.   1,896 m = _____ km _____ m

11.   2,065 m = _____ km _____ m

12.   7,080 m = _____ km _____ m

13.   4,002 m = _____ km _____ m

14.   2,008 m = _____ km _____ m

Look at the map. Then fill in the blanks.

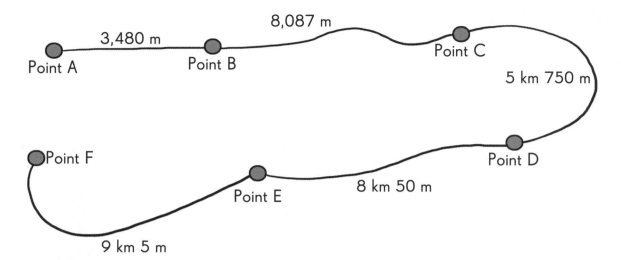

15. Point A is _____ kilometers _____ meters from Point B.

16. Point B is _____ kilometers _____ meters from Point C.

17. Point C is _____ meters from Point D.

18. Point D is _____ meters from Point E.

19. Point E is _____ meters from Point F.

1 km = 1,000 m

Look at the map. Then fill in the blanks.

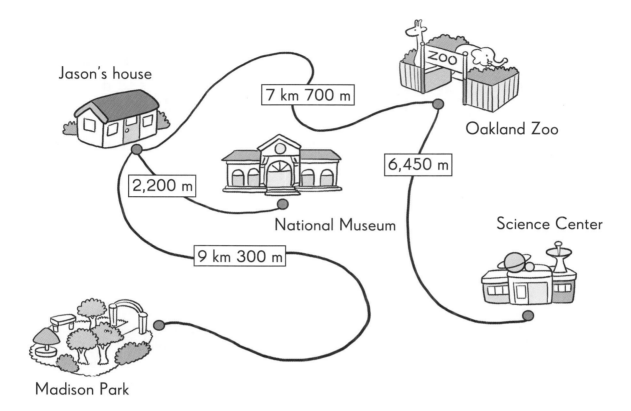

20. The distance between Jason's house and Madison Park

is _____ meters.

21. Jason travels _____ meters from his house to Oakland Zoo.

22. The distance between Oakland Zoo and the Science Center is

_____ kilometers _____ meters.

23. Jason's house is _____ kilometers _____ meters away from the National Museum.

Read the story. Complete the map. Then check (✓) the correct statement.

> The library is 2 kilometers 350 meters from May's house. She cycles to the library every Saturday morning. Then, she goes to the mall to have lunch. The mall is 600 meters from the library.
>
> After lunch, May cycles to a park that is 1 kilometer 65 meters from the mall. In the evening, she cycles 1,800 meters home from the park.

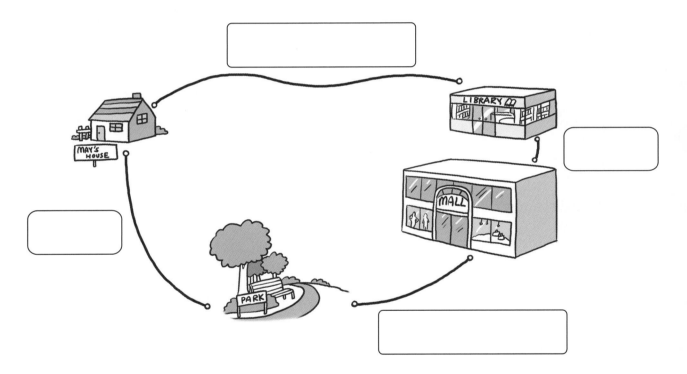

24. The library is nearer to May's house than the park is.

25. The distance from the park to May's house is farther than the distance from the park to the mall.

26. The mall is nearer to the park than to the library.

Lesson 11.3   Kilograms and Grams

Read the scales. Write the mass.

1.

_____ g

2.

_____ kg _____ g

3.

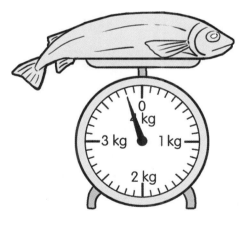

_____ kg _____ g

4.

_____ kg _____ g

Name: _____ **Date:** _____

Write in grams.

5. 6 kg = _____ g

6. 3 kg 438 g = _____ g

7. 8 kg 260 g = _____ g

8. 2 kg 370 g = _____ g

9. 4 kg 50 g = _____ g

10. 5 kg 90 g = _____ g

11. 7 kg 5 g = _____ g

12. 9 kg 8 g = _____ g

Write in kilograms and grams.

13. 3,000 g = _____ kg

14. 2,850 g = _____ kg _____ g

15. 5,643 g = _____ kg _____ g

16. 1,865 g = _____ kg _____ g

17. 3,080 g = _____ kg _____ g

18. 7,055 g = _____ kg _____ g

19. 8,005 g = _____ kg _____ g

| 1 kg = 1,000 g |

20. 9,018 g = _____ kg _____ g

Name: _____ Date: _____

Look at the pictures. The mass of each item is listed on its packaging. Then complete the table and fill in the blanks for Exercises 21 to 25.

cheese

baked beans

rice

peaches

detergent

veggie chips

cereal

milk formula

crabs

cherries

21.

Less than 500 g	More than 500 g but less than 1 kg	From 1 kg to 1 kg 500 g	More than 1 kg 500 g
cheese			

Use the table on the previous page to complete the statements.

22. The _____ is the lightest.

23. The _____ is the heaviest.

24. _____ items are lighter than a jar of cherries.

25. _____ items are heavier than a bag of crabs.

Complete.

26. Order the masses from heaviest to lightest.

2 kg 300 g   3,450 g   1,280 g

_____   _____   _____
heaviest

Lesson 11.4   Liters and Milliliters

Find the volume of water in each measuring cup.

1.

_____ mL

2.

_____ mL

3.

_____ mL

4.

_____ mL

Find the capacity of each container.

5.

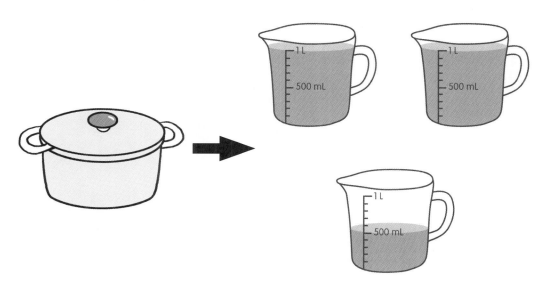

The capacity of the pot is _____ liters _____ milliliters.

6.

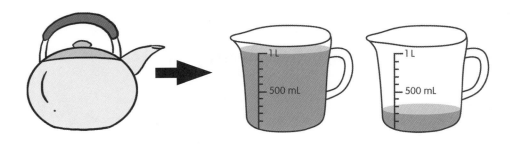

The capacity of the kettle is _____ liter _____ milliliters.

Write in milliliters.

7.   3 L 250 mL = _____ mL

8.   4 L 600 mL = _____ mL

9.   2 L 80 mL = _____ mL

10.   6 L 70 mL = _____ mL

11.   1 L 9 mL = _____ mL

12.   5 L 6 mL = _____ mL

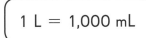

Write in liters and milliliters.

13.   1,800 mL = _____ L _____ mL

14.   2,130 mL = _____ L _____ mL

15.   3,550 mL = _____ L _____ mL

16.   4,090 mL = _____ L _____ mL

17.   6,000 mL = _____ L _____ mL

18.   5,008 mL = _____ L _____ mL

Name: _____ **Date:** _____

Use the clues to answer Exercises 19 and 20.

CLUES

Container F has the largest capacity.
Container E has the smallest capacity.
Container A has a larger capacity than Container C.
Container B has a smaller capacity than Container D
but a larger capacity than Container A.

Match.

19.

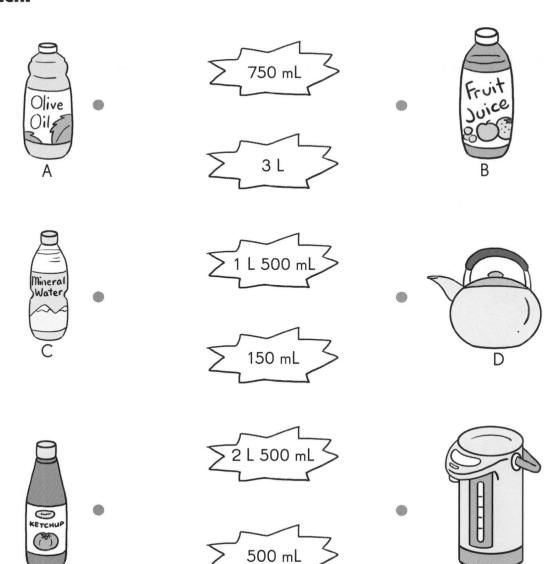

Order the containers by capacity from smallest to largest.

20.   smallest _____E_____

   _____

   _____

   _____

   _____

   largest   _____

Fill in the blanks with *more than*, *less than*, or *equal to*.

21.   2 L 360 mL is _____ 2,360 mL.

22.   4 L 400 mL is _____ 4,040 mL.

23.   7 L 362 mL is _____ 7,632 mL.

24.   8 L 5 mL is _____ 8,050 mL.

25.   9,389 mL is _____ 9 L 389 mL.

26.   10 L 580 mL is _____ 10 L 508 mL.

 **Put on Your Thinking Cap!**

Complete.

The picture shows the distance traveled by each robot.

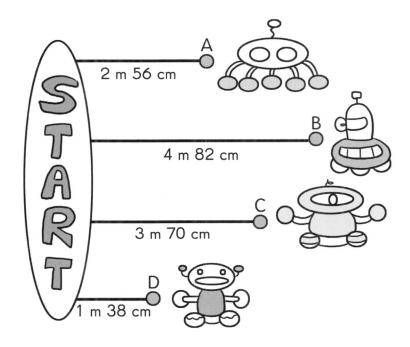

1. Robot C moves _____ centimeters more than Robot A.

2. Robot A moves _____ centimeters less than Robot B.

3. Robot _____ moves the longest distance.

4. Robot _____ moves the shortest distance.

5. The difference between the shortest distance and the longest

distance is _____ centimeters.

Look at the picture. Then complete Exercises 6 to 9.

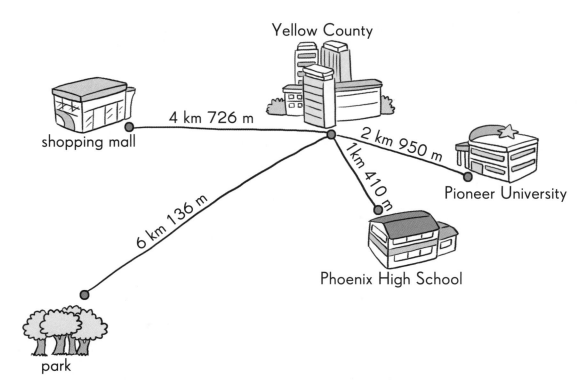

6.   John lives in Yellow County.

     He travels _____ fewer meters to Phoenix High School

     than to the shopping mall.

7.   The _____ is the farthest place from Yellow County.

8.   The _____ is the nearest place to Yellow County.

9.   The difference between the longest and shortest distances from

     Yellow County is _____ meters.

Real-World Problems: Measurement

Lesson 12.1   Real-World Problems: One-Step Problems

Solve. Draw bar models to help you.

1.   Hannah jogs 2,853 meters.
      Kevin jogs 1,670 meters more than Hannah.
      How far does Kevin jog?
      Give your answer in kilometers and meters.

2.   A string is cut into 7 equal pieces. Each piece is
      90 centimeters long. How long was the string at first?
      Give your answer in meters and centimeters.

3. A truck can carry up to 207 kilograms of cargo.
A brick has a mass of 4 kilograms.
What is the maximum number of bricks the truck can carry?

4. A fish tank contains 4,130 milliliters of water.
The tank's capacity is 9 liters 550 milliliters.
How much water is needed to fill the tank completely?
Give your answer in liters and milliliters.

Lesson 12.2   Real-World Problems: Two-Step Problems

Solve. Draw bar models to help you.

1.   The mass of a cow is 540 kilograms.
The cow is 4 times as heavy as a pig.
What is their total mass?

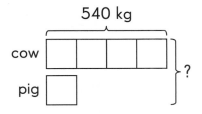

2.   A chef has 4 bottles of cooking oil.
Each bottle contains 2 liters of oil.
How much cooking oil does the chef use if he has
1,365 milliliters of oil left after a week?
Give your answer in liters and milliliters.

3. There are 8 bottles. A nurse pours 100 milliliters of medicine into each bottle. There are still 2,880 milliliters of medicine left.

    a. How much medicine is there in the 8 bottles?
    b. How much medicine is there in all?
Give your answers in liters and milliliters.

4. Glen runs 4 times around a jogging track.
Jamal runs 3 times around the same track.
Glen runs a distance of 992 meters.
How far does Jamal run?

5.   A basket has a watermelon and a bunch of grapes in it.
The watermelon has a mass of 1,460 grams. The bunch of
grapes has a mass of 850 grams. The total mass of the basket and
the fruits is 3 kilograms 50 grams.

   a.   What is the total mass of the watermelon and the bunch of grapes?
Give your answer in kilograms and grams.

   b.   What is the mass of the basket?

6. The total capacity of jugs A and B is 5 liters 330 milliliters.
Jug A holds 850 milliliters more water than Jug B.
What is the capacity of Jug B?
Give your answer in milliliters.

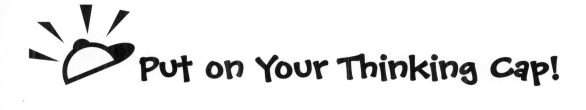 Put on Your Thinking Cap!

1. Jane is 19 centimeters shorter than Mariah.
    Rebecca is 9 centimeters taller than Mariah.
    Find the difference in height between Jane and
    Rebecca.

2. Madison Avenue is 8 kilometers 586 meters long.
Park Avenue is 3 kilometers 795 meters shorter than Madison Avenue.
Lexington Avenue is 4 kilometers 134 meters longer than Park Avenue.

    a. How long is Park Avenue?

    b. Which road is longer, Madison Avenue or Lexington Avenue?
       How much longer is it?

Bar Graphs and Line Plots

Lesson 13.1   Making Bar Graphs with Scales

The picture graph shows the favorite shapes of some students in a school.

Favorite Shapes

Circle	Square	Triangle	Rectangle	Heart

Key: Each ☺ stands for 3 children.

1.   Use the picture graph to draw the bar graph.

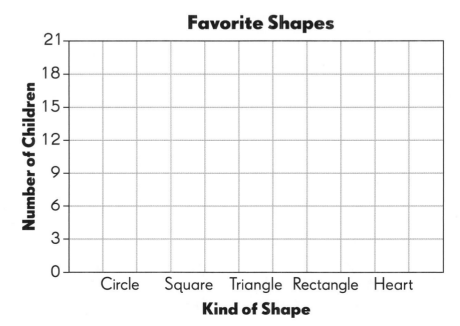

Favorite Shapes

Kevin and his friends collect different kinds of model vehicles.

Kind of Model Vehicle	Tally	Number of Model Vehicles
Motorcycle	⳾卌 卌 |||	13
Truck	|||	3
Bus	卌		6
Bicycle	卌	5
Car	卌 卌 卌 |||	18

2.   Use the information above to draw a bar graph.

Model Vehicles Collected

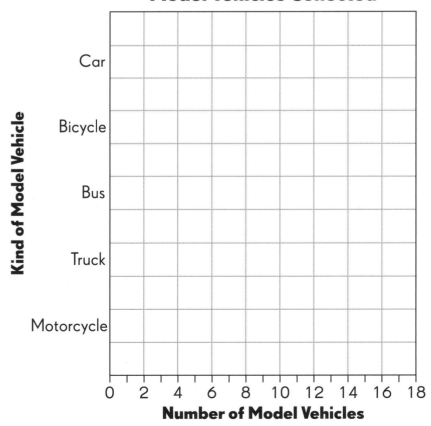

Lesson 13.2   Reading and Interpreting Bar Graphs

The bar graph shows the flavors of breakfast bars that some children like most.
Use the bar graph to answer questions 1 to 5.

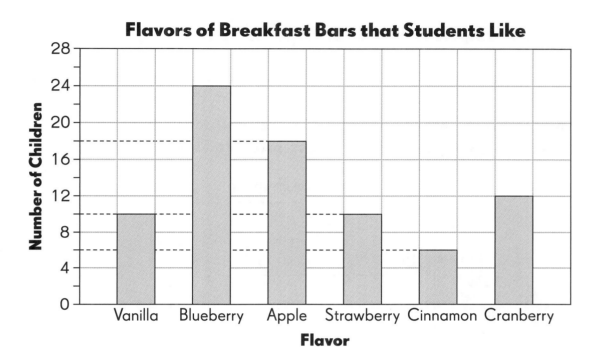

Flavors of Breakfast Bars that Students Like

1.   How many children like cranberry flavored breakfast bars?

_____

2.   How many more children like apple flavored breakfast bars than vanilla flavored breakfast bars?

_____

3.   What is the total number of children who like strawberry flavored breakfast bars and blueberry flavored breakfast bars?

_____

4. What is the difference between the number of children who like the most popular breakfast bar and the number of children who like the least popular breakfast bar?

_____

5. How many children took part in the survey?

_____

**The bar graph shows the kinds of fruits children like.
Use the bar graph to answer questions 6 to 11.**

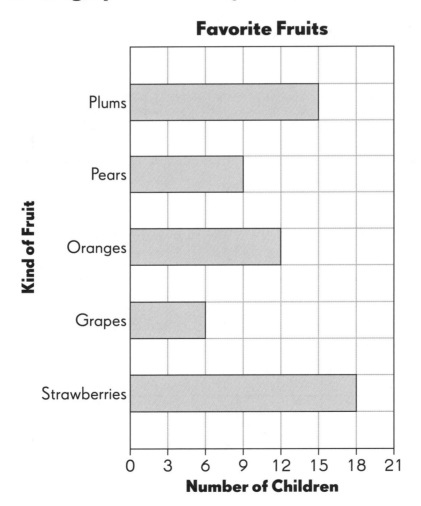

Favorite Fruits

6. How many children like strawberries and oranges?

_____

7. Which fruit is twice as popular as pears?

_____

8. How many more children like the most popular fruit than the least popular fruit?

_____

9. How many fewer children like grapes than plums?

_____

10. The total number of children who like _____ and

_____ is the same as the number of children who like strawberries.

11. Which of the above fruits do you like the most? Why do you like it?

_____

_____

_____

The bar graph shows the favorite colors of a group of students. Use the bar graph to answer questions 12 to 15.

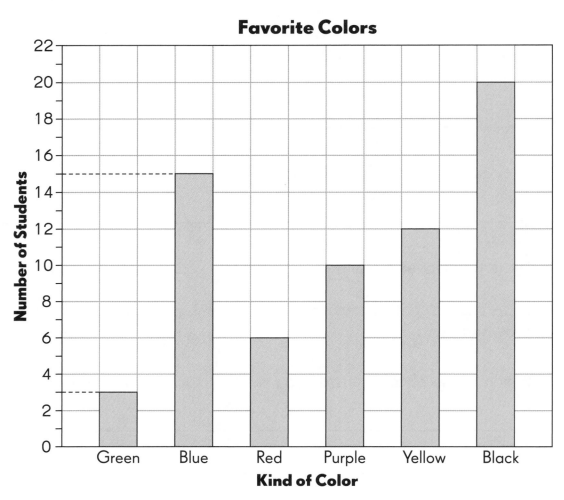

Favorite Colors

12. Four times as many students like _____ as green.

13. How many students like blue, red, or yellow in all?

_____

14. What is the difference between the number of students who like the most popular color and the number of students who like the least popular color?

_____

15. Together, 5 more students like _____ and

_____ than black.

The bar graph shows the number of tourists who visited five places of interest in the United States in a week. Use the bar graph to answer questions 16 to 21.

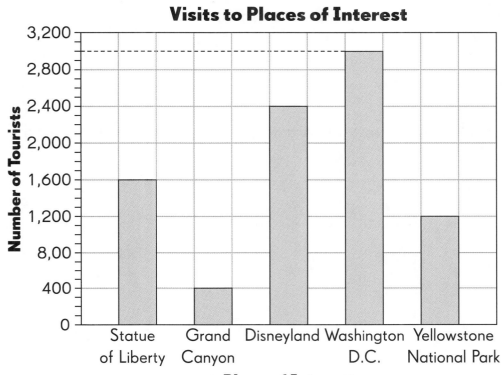

Visits to Places of Interest

16. How many tourists visited the five places altogether?

_____

17. Which place had the least number of tourists?

_____

18. Which place had the greatest number of tourists?

_____

19.   How many more tourists went to Disneyland than the Statue of Liberty?

_____

20.   Which place of interest had twice the number of tourists visiting than Yellowstone National Park had?

_____

21.   Which place of interest had 4 times as many tourists as the Grand Canyon?

_____

Lesson 13.3 Line Plots

The tally chart shows the number of gold medals won by the elementary schools in a district.
Complete the tally chart.

1.   **Gold Medals Won**

Number of Gold Medals	Tally	Number of Schools
1	~~IIII~~ I	
2	III	
3	~~IIII~~ ~~IIII~~	
4	~~IIII~~	

2.   Use the data in the tally chart to make a line plot. Remember to give your line plot a title.

Answer each question. Use the data in your line plot.

3. How many schools are in the district?

_____

4. How many schools won 4 gold medals?

_____

5. How many more schools won 3 gold medals than 1 gold medal?

_____

The list shows the number of laps a group of children jogged around the track.

Number of laps – 2, 3, 4, 2, 2, 6, 6, 5, 5, 5, 2, 5, 2, 2, 2, 2, 2, 3, 4, 4, 3, 2, 3, 3, 3, 2, 2, 4, 4, 4, 4, 4.

6. Complete the table.

Number of Laps	Number of Children
2	
3	
4	
5	
6	

7. Show the data in a line plot. Remember to give your line plot a title.

Answer each question. Use the data in your line plot.

8. How many children jogged 5 laps?

_____

9. How many children jogged more than 3 laps?

_____

10. What is the difference between the number of children who jogged the most laps and the number of children who jogged the fewest laps?

_____

11. How many children took part in the survey?

_____

12. _____ as many children jogged 2 laps as 3 laps.

13. Three times as many children jogged _____ laps as

_____ laps.

The table shows the points students earned in a math test.

Points	Number of Students
6	3
7	4
8	6
9	5
10	2

Line Plot A

Line Plot B

Line Plot C

Line Plot D

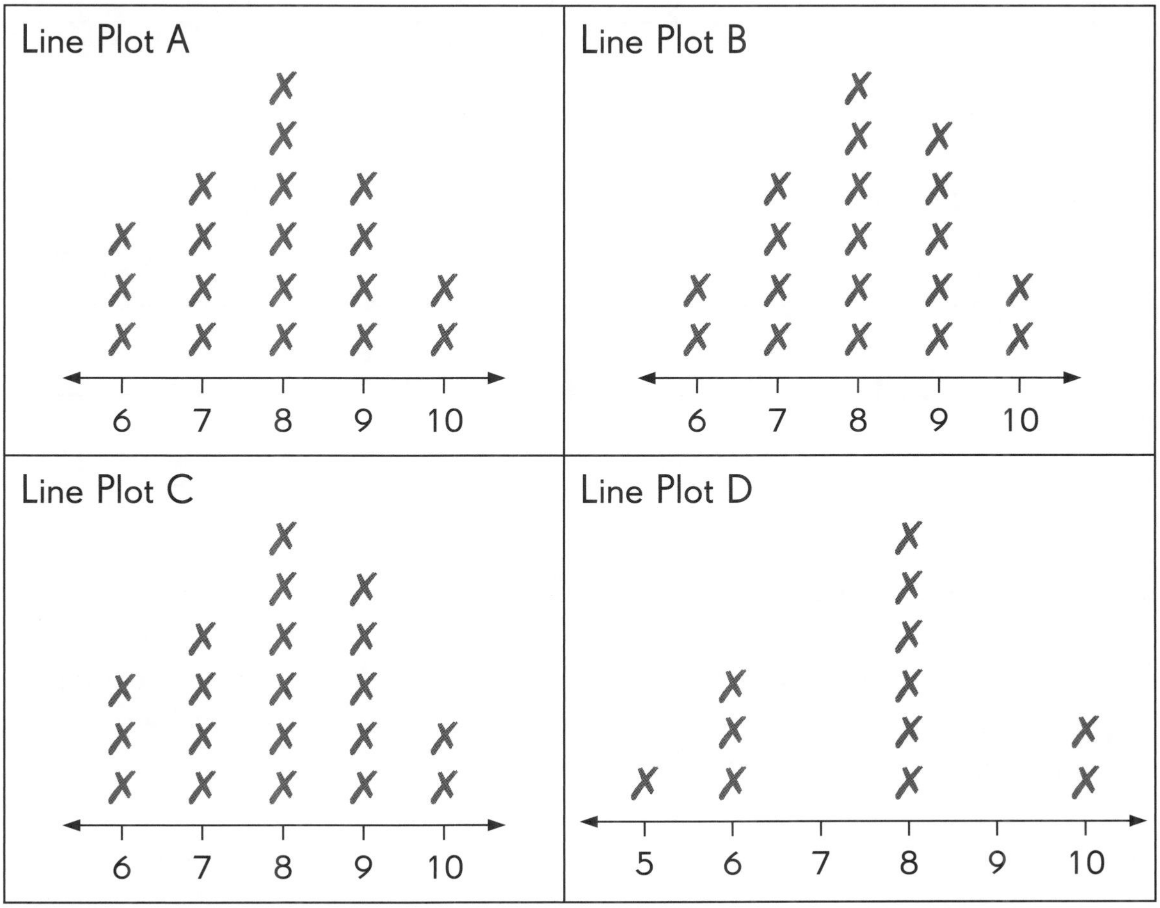

Fill in the blank.
Use the data in the table on page 48.

14.   Line plot _____ matches the given data.

Explain the mistakes in the other line plots.

15.   _____

_____

_____

Name: ______________________ Date: ______________

16. ______________________

____

____

17. ______________________

____

____

Answer the question.

18. A survey asks 150 people how many pets they have. All the people answer 0, 1, 2, 3, 4, or 5. Would a line plot be a good way to show this data? Explain your thinking.

____

____

____

____

Put on Your Thinking Cap!

Study the graph carefully and answer questions 1 to 7.

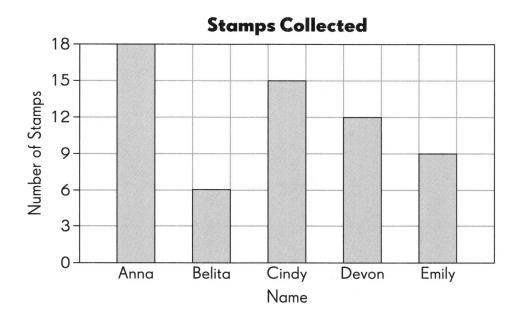

Stamps Collected

1. How many more stamps does Cindy have than Emily?

   _____

2. Name the children who have collected less than 12 stamps.

   _____

3. Who has three times as many stamps as Belita?

   _____

   _____

4. Who has half as many stamps as Devon?

_____

_____

5. Do you think that, together, Anna and Emily will be able to collect 30 stamps? Why or why not?

_____

6. How many more stamps does the girl with the most stamps have than the girl with the fewest stamps?

_____

_____

7. If all 5 girls share the stamps equally,

a. how many stamps would each of them have?

_____

_____

b. how many stamps would Anna have to give away?

_____

_____

 CHAPTER **14** **Fractions**

Lesson 14.1   Understanding Fractions

What fractions make a whole?
Fill in the blanks.

1.

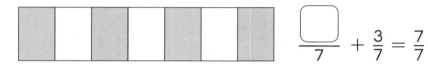

$$\frac{\boxed{}}{7} + \frac{3}{7} = \frac{7}{7}$$

_____-sevenths and _____-sevenths make 1 whole.

What fraction of each figure is shaded?
Fill in each box with the missing numerator.

2.   (e)   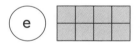 $\dfrac{\boxed{}}{8}$ (c) $\dfrac{\boxed{}}{4}$

(r) $\dfrac{\boxed{}}{5}$ (a)    $\dfrac{\boxed{}}{12}$

(s) $\dfrac{\boxed{}}{8}$ (u)    $\dfrac{\boxed{}}{3}$

(q) $\dfrac{\boxed{}}{6}$ (k)   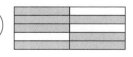 $\dfrac{\boxed{}}{10}$

Match the letters in Exercise 2 with the answers to solve the riddle.

Put three ducks in a box.
What do you have?

A box of ____ ____ ____ ____ ____ ____ ____ ____
(2)   (1)   (5)   (3)   (7)   (8)   (4)   (6)

What fraction of each figure is shaded?
Fill in each box with the missing denominator.

3.

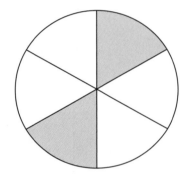

$$\frac{2}{\boxed{}}$$

4.

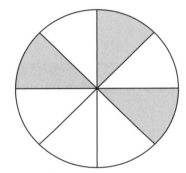

$$\frac{3}{\boxed{}}$$

5.

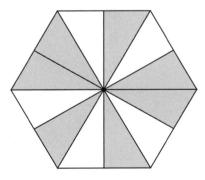

$$\frac{7}{\boxed{}}$$

6.

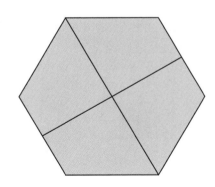

$$\frac{4}{\boxed{}}$$

Lesson 14.2   Understanding Equivalent Fractions

Cut out the fraction pieces on pages 59 and 61.
Then place them on the unit square to help you find the
equivalent fractions.

Unit square

1 whole

Example $\dfrac{1}{2} = \dfrac{\boxed{}}{6}$

Step 1   Place a $\dfrac{1}{2}$-piece on the unit square.

Step 2   Next, completely cover the $\dfrac{1}{2}$-piece with $\dfrac{1}{6}$-pieces.

Step 3   Note the number of $\dfrac{1}{6}$-pieces needed to cover the $\dfrac{1}{2}$-piece
completely.

Answer: Three $\dfrac{1}{6}$-pieces are needed to cover the $\dfrac{1}{2}$-piece completely.

$$\frac{1}{2} = \frac{3}{6}$$

Fill in the missing numerator or denominator.

1. $\dfrac{1}{6} = \dfrac{\boxed{}}{12}$

2. $\dfrac{1}{4} = \dfrac{2}{\boxed{}}$

3. $\dfrac{1}{3} = \dfrac{\boxed{}}{6}$

4. $\dfrac{1}{2} = \dfrac{4}{\boxed{}}$

5. $\dfrac{3}{4} = \dfrac{\boxed{}}{8}$

6. $\dfrac{2}{5} = \dfrac{\boxed{}}{10}$

7. $\dfrac{2}{3} = \dfrac{\boxed{}}{12}$

8. $\dfrac{5}{6} = \dfrac{\boxed{}}{12}$

9. $\dfrac{4}{5} = \dfrac{8}{\boxed{}}$

10. $\dfrac{3}{4} = \dfrac{9}{\boxed{}}$

11. $\dfrac{2}{6} = \dfrac{4}{\boxed{}}$

12. $\dfrac{2}{3} = \dfrac{6}{\boxed{}}$

Name: _____ **Date:** _____

Use different colors to color the mat below to show the fractions $\frac{1}{2}, \frac{1}{3}, \frac{1}{4}, \frac{1}{5}, \frac{1}{6}, \frac{1}{8}, \frac{1}{10}$, and $\frac{1}{12}$.

13.

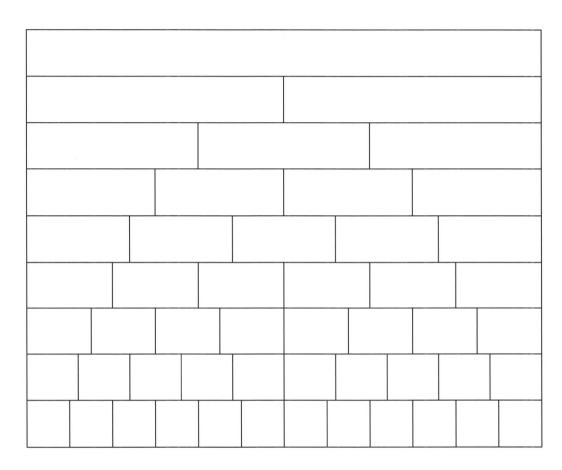

Look at the mat above and circle the pairs of fractions that are equivalent fractions.

14. $\frac{1}{5}$ and $\frac{2}{10}$

15. $\frac{2}{3}$ and $\frac{5}{6}$

16. $\frac{2}{4}$ and $\frac{5}{8}$

17. $\frac{1}{2}$ and $\frac{5}{10}$

18. $\frac{2}{5}$ and $\frac{4}{10}$

19. $\frac{1}{4}$ and $\frac{6}{12}$

20. $\frac{3}{4}$ and $\frac{6}{8}$

21. $\frac{2}{3}$ and $\frac{4}{6}$

Use the number lines to find the equivalent fractions.
Fill in the missing numerators.

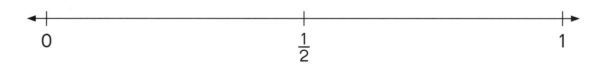

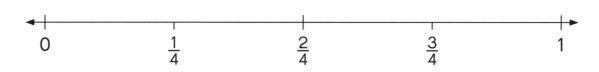

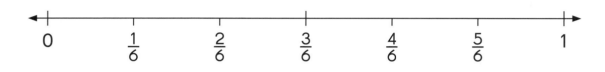

22. $\dfrac{1}{2} = \dfrac{\boxed{}}{4} = \dfrac{\boxed{}}{6} = \dfrac{\boxed{}}{12}$

23. $\dfrac{3}{4} = \dfrac{\boxed{}}{12}$

24. $\dfrac{2}{3} = \dfrac{\boxed{}}{6} = \dfrac{\boxed{}}{12}$

25. $\dfrac{5}{6} = \dfrac{\boxed{}}{12}$

Fraction Pieces

Halves

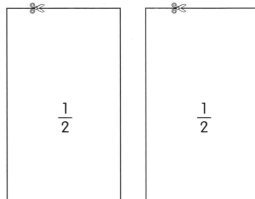

$\frac{1}{2}$ $\frac{1}{2}$

Fourths

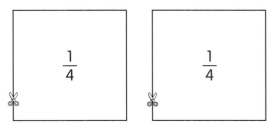

$\frac{1}{4}$ $\frac{1}{4}$

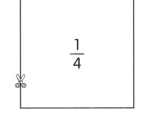

$\frac{1}{4}$ $\frac{1}{4}$

Thirds

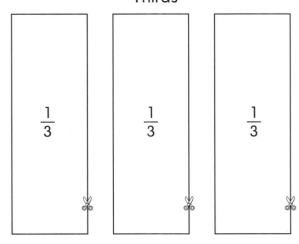

$\frac{1}{3}$ $\frac{1}{3}$ $\frac{1}{3}$

Fifths

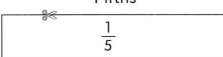

$\frac{1}{5}$

$\frac{1}{5}$

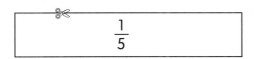

$\frac{1}{5}$

$\frac{1}{5}$

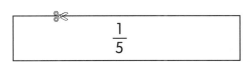

$\frac{1}{5}$

BLANK

Sixths

✂	$\dfrac{1}{6}$

✂	$\dfrac{1}{6}$

✂	$\dfrac{1}{6}$

✂	$\dfrac{1}{6}$

✂	$\dfrac{1}{6}$

✂	$\dfrac{1}{6}$

Eighths

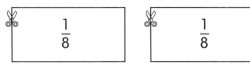

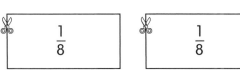

 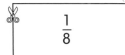

Tenths

✂	$\frac{1}{10}$

✂	$\frac{1}{10}$

✂	$\frac{1}{10}$

✂	$\frac{1}{10}$

✂	$\frac{1}{10}$

✂	$\frac{1}{10}$

✂	$\frac{1}{10}$

✂	$\frac{1}{10}$

✂	$\frac{1}{10}$

✂	$\frac{1}{10}$

Twelfths

✂	$\frac{1}{12}$

✂	$\frac{1}{12}$

✂	$\frac{1}{12}$

✂	$\frac{1}{12}$

✂	$\frac{1}{12}$

✂	$\frac{1}{12}$

✂	$\frac{1}{12}$

✂	$\frac{1}{12}$

✂	$\frac{1}{12}$

✂	$\frac{1}{12}$

✂	$\frac{1}{12}$

✂	$\frac{1}{12}$

BLANK

Lesson 14.3   More Equivalent Fractions

Write the missing numerator, denominator, and fraction.

1.

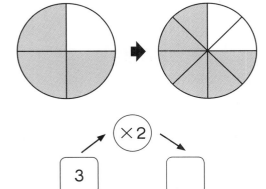

$\dfrac{3}{4}$ is equivalent to $\boxed{}$.

Find the missing numerators and denominators.

2.   ×2 $\dfrac{2}{5} = \dfrac{\boxed{}}{\boxed{}}$ ×2

3.   ×4 $\dfrac{1}{3} = \dfrac{\boxed{}}{\boxed{}}$ ×4

4.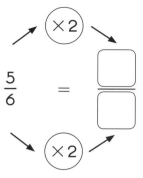

$$\frac{3}{4} = \frac{\boxed{}}{\boxed{}}$$

5.

$$\frac{5}{6} = \frac{\boxed{}}{\boxed{}}$$

Find the missing numerators or denominators.

6. $\dfrac{4}{5} = \dfrac{\boxed{}}{10}$

7. $\dfrac{1}{2} = \dfrac{6}{\boxed{}}$

8. $\dfrac{2}{3} = \dfrac{6}{\boxed{}}$

9. $\dfrac{2}{9} = \dfrac{4}{\boxed{}}$

10. $\dfrac{3}{4} = \dfrac{\boxed{}}{8} = \dfrac{\boxed{}}{12} = \dfrac{\boxed{}}{16}$

11. $\dfrac{3}{3} = \dfrac{6}{\boxed{}} = \dfrac{9}{\boxed{}} = \dfrac{12}{\boxed{}}$

12. $\dfrac{3}{5} = \dfrac{\boxed{}}{10} = \dfrac{\boxed{}}{15} = \dfrac{\boxed{}}{20}$

Draw to show the simplest fraction.
Then write the fraction in the boxes.

Example

$$\frac{4}{8} = \frac{1}{2}$$

÷ 4

÷ 4

$\frac{4}{8}$ is equivalent to $\boxed{\frac{1}{2}}$.

13.

$$\frac{8}{10} = \frac{4}{\boxed{}}$$

÷ 2

÷ 2

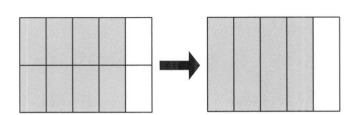

$\frac{8}{10}$ is equivalent to $\boxed{}$.

Find the missing numerators and denominators.

14.

$$\frac{9}{12} = \frac{\boxed{}}{\boxed{}}$$

÷ 3

÷ 3

15.

$$\frac{3}{9} = \frac{\boxed{}}{\boxed{}}$$

÷ 3

÷ 3

16.

$$\frac{5}{10} = \frac{\boxed{}}{\boxed{}}$$

÷ 5

÷ 5

17.

$$\frac{6}{8} = \frac{\boxed{}}{\boxed{}}$$

÷ 2

÷ 2

Write each fraction in simplest form.

18. $\dfrac{2}{6} = \dfrac{\boxed{}}{\boxed{}}$

19. $\dfrac{4}{8} = \dfrac{\boxed{}}{\boxed{}}$

20. $\dfrac{6}{10} = \dfrac{\boxed{}}{\boxed{}}$

21. $\dfrac{8}{10} = \dfrac{\boxed{}}{\boxed{}}$

22. $\dfrac{3}{12} = \dfrac{\boxed{}}{\boxed{}}$

23. $\dfrac{9}{12} = \dfrac{\boxed{}}{\boxed{}}$

24. $\dfrac{8}{12} = \dfrac{\boxed{}}{\boxed{}}$

25. $\dfrac{10}{12} = \dfrac{\boxed{}}{\boxed{}}$

26. $\dfrac{2}{8} = \dfrac{\boxed{}}{\boxed{}}$

27. $\dfrac{4}{10} = \dfrac{\boxed{}}{\boxed{}}$

28. $\dfrac{15}{20} = \dfrac{\boxed{}}{\boxed{}}$

29. $\dfrac{6}{9} = \dfrac{\boxed{}}{\boxed{}}$

Lesson 14.4   Comparing Fractions

Compare the fractions.

1. $\frac{5}{7}$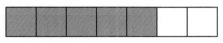

$\frac{1}{2}$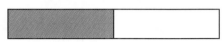

_____ is less than _____.

2.

$\frac{7}{10}$ $\frac{1}{2}$

_____ is greater than _____.

3.

$\frac{5}{7}$ $\frac{2}{7}$

_____ is less than _____.

4.

$\frac{2}{6}$ $\frac{4}{6}$

_____ is greater than _____.

5.

$\frac{4}{7}$

$\frac{4}{5}$

_____ is less than _____.

6.

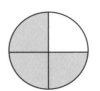

$\frac{3}{10}$

$\frac{3}{4}$

_____ is greater than _____.

Compare the fractions.

7. Which is less, $\frac{2}{3}$ or $\frac{7}{12}$?

$\frac{2}{3} = $ _____

_____ < _____

8. Which is greater, $\frac{5}{8}$ or $\frac{1}{4}$?

$\frac{1}{4} = $ _____

_____ > _____

Change to equivalent like fractions.

9. Which is less, $\frac{2}{3}$ or $\frac{2}{9}$?

$\frac{2}{3} = $ _____

_____ < _____

Compare. Write < or >.

Use $\frac{1}{2}$ as a benchmark.

10.

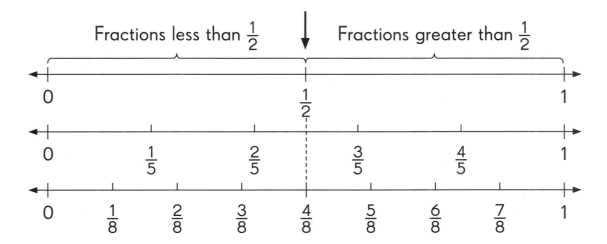

$\frac{2}{5}$ ◯ $\frac{1}{2}$

$\frac{5}{8}$ ◯ $\frac{1}{2}$

So, $\frac{2}{5}$ ◯ $\frac{5}{8}$.

Compare the fractions. Fill in the blanks.

11. $\frac{1}{3}$ and $\frac{2}{3}$

_____ is greater.

12. $\frac{4}{5}$ and $\frac{6}{10}$

_____ is greater.

13. $\frac{10}{11}$ and $\frac{1}{2}$

_____ is greater.

14. $\frac{4}{7}$ and $\frac{4}{8}$

_____ is greater.

Order the fractions from least to the greatest.

15. $\frac{1}{2}$, $\frac{1}{4}$, $\frac{1}{6}$ _____

16. $\frac{3}{4}$, $\frac{5}{6}$, $\frac{2}{3}$ _____

17. $\frac{3}{4}$, $\frac{7}{12}$, $\frac{2}{6}$ _____

18. $\frac{5}{6}$, $\frac{5}{8}$, $\frac{5}{12}$ _____

Order the fractions from greatest to the least.

19. $\frac{3}{8}$, $\frac{3}{4}$, $\frac{1}{2}$ _____

20. $\frac{1}{6}$, $\frac{1}{3}$, $\frac{1}{9}$ _____

21. $\frac{11}{12}$, $\frac{3}{4}$, $\frac{5}{6}$ _____

22. $\frac{2}{4}$, $\frac{2}{6}$, $\frac{2}{3}$ _____

Name: _____ **Date:** _____

Lesson 14.5 Adding and Subtracting Like Fractions (Part 1)

Complete the model.
Add the fractions.

1.

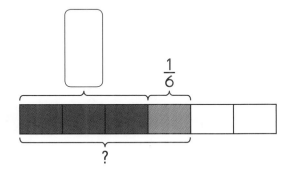

$$\frac{\boxed{}}{6} + \frac{1}{6} = \boxed{}$$

2.

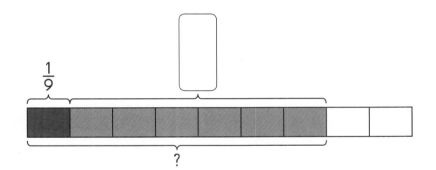

$$\frac{1}{9} + \frac{\boxed{}}{9} = \boxed{}$$

3.

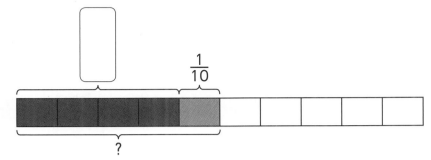

$$\frac{\boxed{}}{10} + \frac{1}{10} = \boxed{}$$

4.

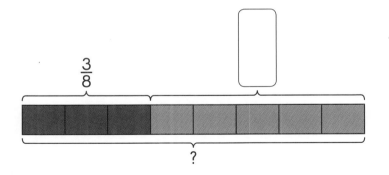

$$\frac{3}{8} + \frac{\boxed{}}{8} = \boxed{}$$

Add.

5. $\frac{1}{2} + \frac{1}{2} =$ ☐

6. $\frac{1}{3} + \frac{2}{3} =$ ☐

7. $\frac{2}{5} + \frac{1}{5} =$ ☐

8. $\frac{1}{6} + \frac{3}{6} =$ ☐

Solve.

9.   What fraction should you add to the sum of $\frac{3}{8}$ and $\frac{3}{8}$ to get 1 whole?   ☐

10.   What fraction should you add to the sum of $\frac{2}{10}$ and $\frac{3}{10}$ to get 1 whole?   ☐

11.   What fraction should you add to the sum of $\frac{2}{9}$ and $\frac{4}{9}$ to get 1 whole?   ☐

Lesson 14.5 Adding and Subtracting Like Fractions (Part 2)

Complete the model.
Subtract the fractions.

1.

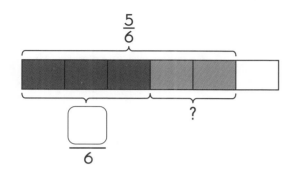

$$\frac{5}{6} - \frac{\boxed{}}{6} = \boxed{}$$

2.

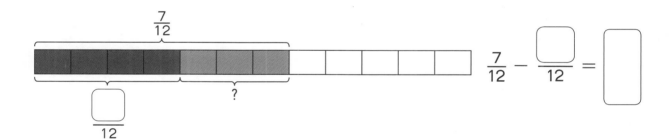

$$\frac{7}{12} - \frac{\boxed{}}{12} = \boxed{}$$

3.

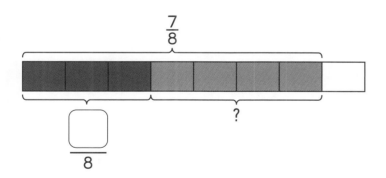

$$\frac{7}{8} - \frac{\boxed{}}{8} = \boxed{}$$

4.

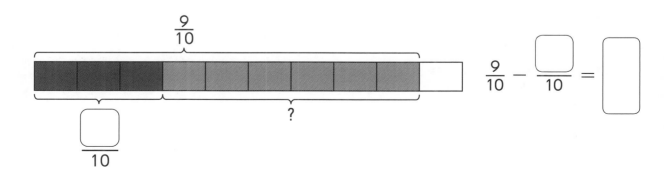

$$\frac{9}{10} - \frac{\boxed{}}{10} = \boxed{}$$

Name: _____ **Date:** _____

Subtract.

5. $\dfrac{5}{8} - \dfrac{2}{8} = \boxed{}$

6. $\dfrac{8}{9} - \dfrac{4}{9} = \boxed{}$

7. $\dfrac{6}{7} - \dfrac{4}{7} = \boxed{}$

8. $\dfrac{7}{11} - \dfrac{2}{11} = \boxed{}$

9. $\dfrac{5}{6} - \dfrac{2}{6} - \dfrac{1}{6} = \boxed{}$

10. $\dfrac{7}{12} - \dfrac{5}{12} - \dfrac{1}{12} = \boxed{}$

11. $1 - \dfrac{3}{4} = \boxed{}$

12. $1 - \dfrac{2}{3} = \boxed{}$

Solve.

13. What fraction should you add to the difference of

$\dfrac{8}{12}$ and $\dfrac{1}{12}$ to get 1 whole? $\boxed{}$

Lesson 14.6   Fraction of a Set
What fraction of each set of objects is shaded?
Fill in the blanks.

1.

_____

2.

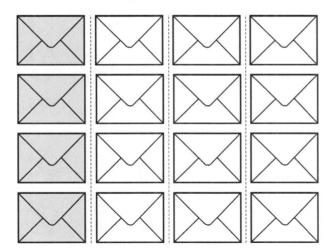

_____

3.

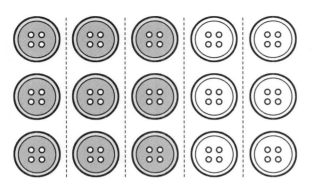

_____

4.

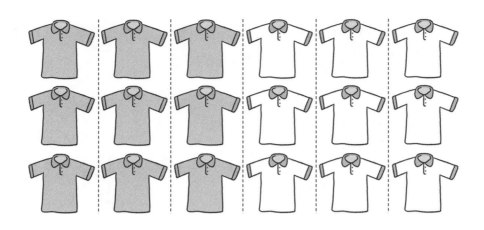

_____

Solve. Use pictures and bar models to help you.

5. $\frac{2}{3}$ of the 12 beetles are brown. How many beetles are brown?

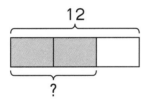

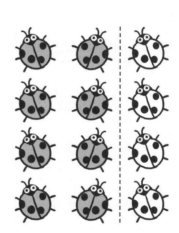

3 units ⟶ 12

1 unit ⟶ ⬚ ÷ ⬚

= ⬚

2 units ⟶ ⬚ × ⬚

= ⬚

$\frac{2}{3}$ of 12 is ⬚.

So, ⬚ of the beetles are brown.

6. $\frac{3}{4}$ of the 16 apples are green.

How many apples are green? ☐

7. $\frac{5}{8}$ of the 24 oranges were eaten.

How many oranges were eaten? ☐

8. $\frac{4}{7}$ of the 21 breakfast bars are vanilla flavored.

How many breakfast bars are vanilla flavored?   ☐

9. $\frac{2}{3}$ of the 60 shirts are blue.

How many shirts are blue?   ☐

Put on Your Thinking Cap!

Shade the two fractions in each model and solve the problem.

1. Maria bought 1 liter of mango juice.

She used $\frac{3}{8}$ liter of the juice on the first day and $\frac{1}{4}$ liter on the second day.

How much mango juice is left at the end of the second day?

2. What fraction of each square is shaded?

a.
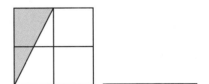
_____

b.
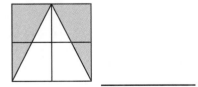
_____

c.

_____

d.
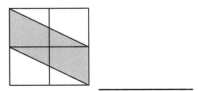
_____

e.

_____

f.
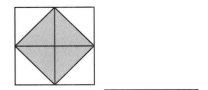
_____

Solve. Draw models to help you.

3.   Box X and Box Y are the same size.

$\frac{2}{3}$ of Box X contains sand and $\frac{2}{9}$ of Box Y contains sand.

How much sand from Box X must be poured into Box Y so that the boxes

contain the same amount of sand?

4.   Alvin had $\frac{5}{6}$ of a pizza.

Tom had a part of an equal-sized pizza.

Alvin gave $\frac{1}{6}$ of his pizza to Tom.

Now, both of them have the same amount of pizza.

What fraction of a pizza did Tom have at first?

CHAPTER 15 Customary Length, Weight, and Capacity

Lesson 15.1   Measuring Length

Measure each object to the nearest inch.

1.

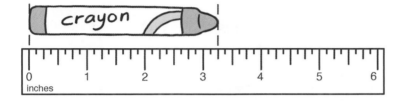

The crayon is about _____ inches long.

2.

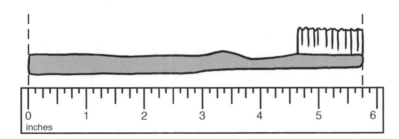

The toothbrush is about _____ inches long.

3.

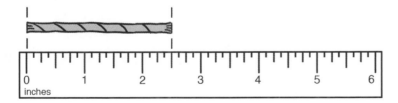

The rope is about _____ inches long.

Measure each object to the nearest half-inch.

4.

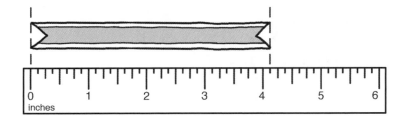

The ribbon is about _____ inches long.

5.

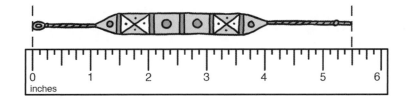

The friendship band is about _____ inches long.

6.

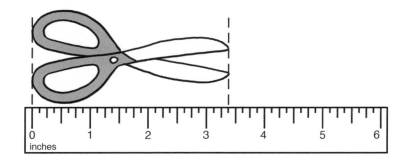

The scissors are about _____ inches long.

7.

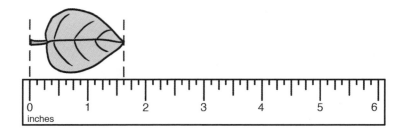

The leaf is about _____ inches long.

3500

8.

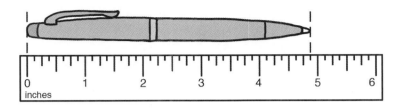

The pen is about _____ inches long.

Estimate the length of the ribbon to the nearest inch.

Each quarter dollar is about one inch wide.

9. The ribbon is about _____
quarters long.

10. It is about _____ inches long.

Estimate the length of the bracelet to the nearest half-inch.

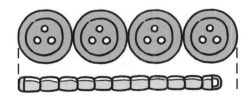

Each button is about a half-inch wide.

11. The bracelet is about _____
buttons long.

12. It is about _____ inches long.

Fill in the blanks.

13.   1 ft = _____ in.

14.   1 yd = _____ ft

                = _____ in.

Circle the best estimate for each.

15.   The length of a book

            a. 10 in.   **b.** 2 ft

16.   The height of a house

            a. 18 ft   **b.** 18 in.

17. The length of a bed

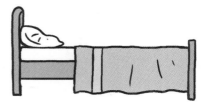

a. 6 yd   **b.** 6 ft

18. The length of a hiking trail

a. 10 yd   **b.** 5 mi

Complete.
Use the map to help you.

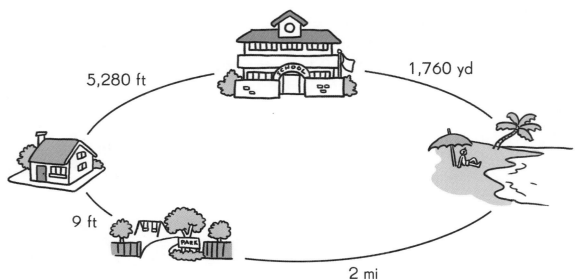

5,280 ft

1,760 yd

9 ft

2 mi

19. The distance between home and school is about _____ mile.

Use the map on the previous page to answer the exercises.

20. Carol can walk 1 mile in 20 minutes. How long will it take her to walk from school to the beach?

_____ minutes

21. The distance between home and the park is _____ yards.

22. How much time does Carol need to walk between the park and the beach?

_____ minutes

Choose the unit you would use to measure each length. Write *inches*, *feet*, *yards*, or *miles*.

23. The height of a building _____

24. The length of a caterpillar _____

25. The length of an airplane _____

26. The distance between two towns _____

Lesson 15.2   Measuring Weight

Read the scales and write the weights.

1.

The bag of limes weighs

about _____ ounces.

2.

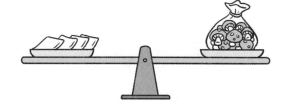

1 slice of cheese weighs about
1 ounce.
The bag of mushrooms weighs

about _____ ounces.

3.

The turkey weighs about

_____ pounds.

4.

The apples weigh about

_____ pounds.

5.

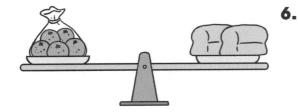

A loaf of bread weighs about
1 pound.
The bag of oranges weighs

about _____ pounds.

6.

The two books weigh about

_____ pounds.

Choose the unit that you would use to measure the weight of each object. Write _ounces_, _pounds_, or _tons_.

7.

You can measure the weight of a

basket of fruits in _____.

8.

You can measure the weight of two

slices of bread in _____.

9.

You can measure the weight of a

polar bear in _____.

10.

You can measure the weight of five

grapes in _____.

11.

You can measure the weight of

two books in _____.

12.

You can measure the weight of a

coach in _____.

Order the weights from the lightest to the heaviest.

13.   8 lb   4 oz   2 T

_____

14.   1 T   3 lb   10 oz

_____

Circle the best estimate for each.

15.   Johnson estimates the weight of 3 apples.
Which is the best estimate of their weight?

a. 5 oz   **b.** 15 oz   **c.** 20 lb   **d.** 10 lb

16. Which is the best estimate of the weight of a puppy?

a. 2 oz   **b.** 200 lb   **c.** 8 lb   **d.** 80 lb

17. Which is the best estimate of the weight of a container of pasta sauce?

a. 2 oz   **b.** 4 lb   **c.** 90 oz   **d.** 14 oz

Choose the best unit to complete the sentences.

> tons   pounds   ounces

18. You can measure the weight of a car in _____.

19. You can measure the weight of a fork in _____.

20. You can measure the weight of a large watermelon in _____.

21. You can measure the weight of a cow in _____.

Lesson 15.3   Measuring Capacity

Find the capacity of each container.

Each 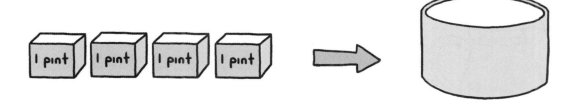 = 1 cup.

1.   The pitcher can hold _____ cups of water.

2.   The pitcher has a capacity of _____ cups.

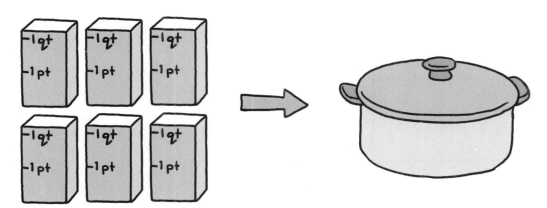

3.   The container can hold _____ pints of milk.

4.   The container has a capacity of _____ pints.

5.   The pot can hold _____ quarts of soup.

6.   The pot has a capacity of _____ quarts.

7. The bathtub can hold _____ gallons of water.

8. The bathtub has a capacity of _____ gallons.

Circle the best estimate for each.

9.

a. 4 pt   **b.** 4 gal

10.

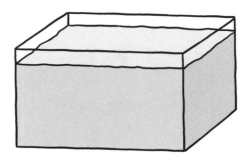

a. 20 qt   **b.** 200 gal

Match. Each = 1 cup.

11.

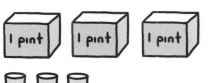
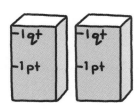

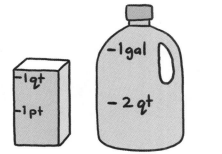

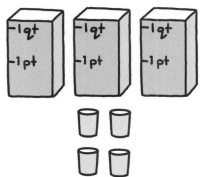
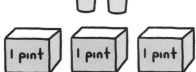

Order the capacities from the smallest to largest.

12. 1 gal   6 pt   8 qt

_____

13. 2 qt   20 c   8 pt

_____

14. 1 qt   8 c   3 pt

_____

15. 1 gal   2 qt   3 pt

_____

Choose the best unit to complete the sentences.

> cups   gallons   pints   quarts

16. You can measure the capacity of a small milk bottle in _____.

17. You can measure the capacity of a kettle in _____.

18. You can measure the capacity of a gas tank in _____.

 Put on Your Thinking Cap!

Solve.

1. The total height of Clifford and Jennifer is 108 inches.
Clifford is 6 inches taller than Jennifer.
How tall is Clifford?

2. There are 5 trees along the side of a road that is 50 yards long.
Tree B is half-way between Tree A and Tree C.
Tree C is half-way between Tree B and Tree D.
Tree D is half-way between Tree B and Tree E.
What is the distance between Tree D and Tree E?

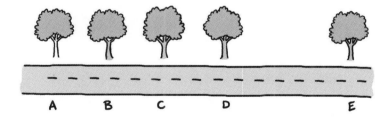

3.   A dog takes 4 steps to walk the same distance that a cat takes 5 steps to walk.
        Each dog step has a length of 1 foot.
        How far does the cat walk when it takes 20 steps?

4.   A kangaroo chases a rabbit that is 120 feet ahead of it.
        For every 5-foot leap the rabbit takes, the kangaroo makes a 15-foot leap.
        How many leaps does the kangaroo need to make to catch up to the rabbit?

Test Prep

50

for Chapters 10 to 15

Multiple Choice (10 × 2 points = 20 points)

Fill in the circle next to the correct answer.

1. Joe has $2.50. He buys a pen for $1.90.
   How much money does he have left?

   Ⓐ 10¢   Ⓑ 50¢   Ⓒ 60¢   Ⓓ $1.60

2. The length of an adult bed is about _____.

   Ⓐ 3 yards   Ⓑ 70 feet

   Ⓒ 7 feet   Ⓓ 7 yards

3. A piece of rope is 409 centimeters long.

   It is _____ long.

   Ⓐ 4 meters 9 centimeters

   Ⓑ 4 meters 90 centimeters

   Ⓒ 40 meters 9 centimeters

   Ⓓ 40 meters 90 centimeters

4. A container has 1 gallon of juice in it. Holly and her friends drink
   8 cups of juice. How many cups of juice are left?

   Ⓐ 10   Ⓑ 8   Ⓒ 6   Ⓓ 4

5.   What is the mass of the melon?

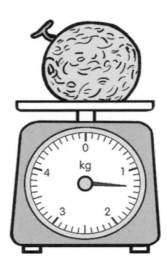

Ⓐ 1 kg 100 g   Ⓑ 1 kg 200 g

Ⓒ 1 kg 300 g   Ⓓ 1 kg 400 g

6.   There is 1 liter 80 milliliters of water in a bottle. The capacity of the bottle is 2 liters. _____ milliliters more water is needed to fill the bottle completely.

Ⓐ 20   Ⓑ 200   Ⓒ 920   Ⓓ 1,920

7.   Which is equivalent to $\frac{2}{5}$?

Ⓐ $\frac{2}{3}$ Ⓑ $\frac{2}{10}$ Ⓒ $\frac{6}{10}$ Ⓓ $\frac{6}{15}$

8.   Find the two fractions which give a sum of 1 and a difference of $\frac{1}{2}$.

Ⓐ $\frac{1}{2}$ and 1   Ⓑ $\frac{3}{4}$ and $\frac{1}{4}$

Ⓒ $\frac{4}{6}$ and $\frac{1}{6}$ Ⓓ $\frac{7}{8}$ and $\frac{3}{8}$

The bar graph shows the favorite fruits of some children. Use the bar graph to answer Exercises 9 and 10.

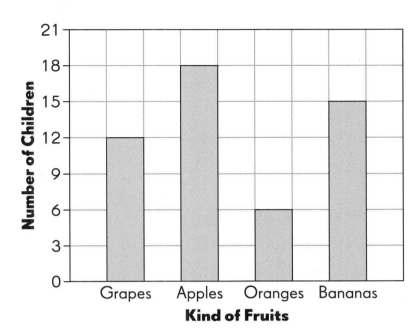

9. How many children like grapes and bananas?

　(A) 20　　　　(B) 24　　　　(C) 27　　　　(D) 30

10. How many more children like apples than oranges?

　(A) 12　　　　(B) 8　　　　(C) 6　　　　(D) 4

Short Answer (10 × 2 points = 20 points)

Write your answer in the space given.

11. How many ounces are there in 4 pounds?

_____ oz

12. Order the fractions from least to greatest.

$$\frac{5}{6} \qquad \frac{7}{12} \qquad \frac{2}{3}$$

_____

13. Bobby is 28 centimeters shorter than Daniel.
Roy is 19 centimeters taller than Daniel.
Find the difference in height between Roy and Bobby.

_____ cm

14. The mass of a duck is 1 kilogram 60 grams.
The duck is 548 grams heavier than a chicken.
What is the mass of the chicken?

_____ g

15. Alicia jogs $\frac{1}{2}$ kilometer and Ivy jogs $\frac{3}{8}$ kilometer.
How many kilometers do they jog altogether?

_____ km

16. A basket has 12 fruits in it. 10 of the fruits are apples.
What fraction of the fruits are apples?

_____

17. Mrs. Lam buys some vegetables for $8.75 and
2 chickens for $6 each. How much does she pay in all?

$_____

18. The capacity of a bottle is 1,380 milliliters.
The capacity of a kettle is 1 liter 200 milliliters more than
the bottle. What is the capacity of the kettle?

_____ mL

19. Stella has a ribbon that is 5 feet long. She uses 28 inches
of it to tie a gift. What is the length of the ribbon
that Stella has left?

_____ in.

20. Jenna has $50. She buys a book and a bag. The book
costs $12.50 and the bag costs $28.80. How much money
does Jenna have left?

$_____

Extended Response (Questions 21 and 22: 2 × 2 = 4 points,
Questions 23 and 24: 3 × 2 = 6 points)

Solve. Show your work.

21. Pail X can hold 5 liters 60 milliliters of water.
It can hold 1,850 milliliters more water than Pail Y.
What is the capacity of Pail Y?
Give your answer in liters and milliliters.

22. Bag P is 5 times as heavy as Bag Q.
Bag Q has a mass of 180 grams.
What is the total mass of Bag P and Bag Q?
Give your answer in kilograms and grams.

23. Road A is 5 kilometers 100 meters long.
Road B is 750 meters shorter than Road A.
Road C is 1,690 meters longer than Road B.
How long is Road C?
Give your answer in kilometers and meters.

24. Barry has $2 less than Alex.
Carl has $3 less than Barry.
They have $35 altogether.
How much money does Barry have?

CHAPTER 16 Time and Temperature

Lesson 16.1   Telling Time

Tell the time. Use *past* or *to*.

Example

11:28

52 minutes past 7   32 minutes to 12

1.

_____

2.

2:32

_____

3.

_____

4.

9:39

_____

Name: _____   **Date:** _____

Tell the time in two ways.

┌─ *Example* ───┐

_____ 2:18 _____   _____ 10:11 _____

__18 minutes past 2__   __49 minutes to 11__

__27 minutes past 8__   __32 minutes past 5__

__33 minutes to 9__   __28 minutes to 6__

└──┘

5.

_____

_____

6.

_____

_____

Fill in each blank with the correct time.

7. 21 minutes past 8 is _____.   **8.** 11 minutes to 11 is _____.

9. 7:18 is _____ minutes past _____.

10. 10:53 is _____ minutes to _____.

Lesson 16.2   Converting Hours and Minutes

Express the time in minutes.

1.   3 h = _____ min

2.   1 h 45 min = _____ min

3.   2 h 29 min = _____ min

4.   4 h 31 min = _____ min

5.   6 h 18 min = _____ min

6.   3 h 23 min = _____ min

7.   2 h 58 min = _____ min

8.   4 h 42 min = _____ min

Express the time in hours.

9.   360 min = _____ h

10.   240 min = _____ h

11.   300 min = _____ h

12.   420 min = _____ h

13.   180 min = _____ h

Express the time in hours and minutes.

14.   95 min = _____ h _____ min

15.   105 min = _____ h _____ min

16.   160 min = _____ h _____ min

17.   195 min = _____ h _____ min

18.   235 min = _____ h _____ min

19.   270 min = _____ h _____ min

20.   305 min = _____ h _____ min

21.   420 min = _____ h _____ min

Solve each word problem.
Show your work.

22.   Sylvia plays basketball for 110 minutes.
How many hours and minutes are there in 110 minutes?

23.   Jack takes 2 hours 35 minutes to complete his science project.
How many minutes are there in 2 hours 35 minutes?

Lesson 16.3   Adding Hours and Minutes

Add.

— *Example* —

1 h 25 min + 2 h 15 min

1 h   25 min   2 h   15 min

So, 1 h 25 min + 2 h 15 min
= 3 h 40 min

Step 1	1 h + 2 h = 3 h
Step 2	25 min + 15 min = 40 min
Step 3	3 h + 40 min = 3 h 40 min

1.   3 h 40 min + 4 h 15 min

3 h   40 min   4 h   15 min

So, 3 h 40 min + 4 h 15 min

= ___ h ___ min

Step 1   ___ h + ___ h = ___ h

Step 2   ___ min + ___ min

= ___ min

Step 3   ___ h + ___ min

= ___ h ___ min

2.   2 h 35 min + 6 h 20 min

2 h   35 min   6 h   20 min

So, 2 h 35 min + 6 h 20 min

= ___ h ___ min

Step 1   ___ h + ___ h = ___ h

Step 2   ___ min + ___ min

= ___ min

Step 3   ___ h + ___ min

= ___ h ___ min

3.   4 h 5 min + 5 h 30 min | Step 1 | ___ h + ___ h = ___ h

4 h   5 min   5 h   30 min | Step 2 | ___ min + ___ min

So, 4 h 5 min + 5 h 30 min   = ___ min

= ___ h ___ min | Step 3 | ___ h + ___ min

                                                      = ___ h ___ min

Add.

4.   **a.**   3 h 18 min + 3 h 35 min = _____ h _____ min

b.   3 h 35 min + 1 h 15 min = _____ h _____ min

c.   4 h 16 min + 2 h 37 min = _____ h _____ min

d.   5 h 24 min + 3 h 39 min = _____ h _____ min

= _____ h _____ min

e.   3 h 45 min + 6 h 30 min = _____ h _____ min

= _____ h _____ min

f.   7 h 40 min + 3 h 25 min = _____ h _____ min

= _____ h _____ min

g.   3 h 29 min + 8 h 48 min = _____ h _____ min

= _____ h _____ min

h.   9 h 15 min + 1 h 50 min = _____ h _____ min

= _____ h _____ min

i.   4 h 48 min + 8 h 42 min = _____ h _____ min

= _____ h _____ min

Lesson 16.4   Subtracting Hours and Minutes

Subtract.

> **Example**
>
> 5 h 40 min − 2 h 15 min
>
> 5 h   40 min   2 h   15 min
>
> So, 5 h 40 min − 2 h 15 min
> = 3 h 25 min
>
> | Step 1 | 5 h − 2 h = 3 h |
> | Step 2 | 40 min − 15 min = 25 min |
> | Step 3 | 3 h + 25 min = 3 h 25 min |

1.   4 h 25 min − 3 h 20 min

4 h   25 min   3 h   20 min

So, 4 h 25 min − 3 h 20 min

= ___ h ___ min

Step 1   ___ h − ___ h = ___ h

Step 2   ___ min − ___ min

= ___ min

Step 3   ___ h + ___ min

= ___ h ___ min

2.   8 h 45 min − 3 h 30 min

8 h   45 min   3 h   30 min

So, 8 h 45 min − 3 h 30 min

= ___ h ___ min

Step 1   ___ h − ___ h = ___ h

Step 2   ___ min − ___ min

= ___ min

Step 3   ___ h + ___ min

= ___ h ___ min

Subtract.

3.   **a.**   10 h 50 min − 3 h 32 min = _____ h _____ min

   b.   15 h 20 min − 7 h 36 min

   = _____ h _____ min − _____ h _____ min

   = _____ h _____ min

   c.   20 h 15 min − 6 h 38 min

   = _____ h _____ min − _____ h _____ min

   = _____ h _____ min

   d.   12 h 30 min − 5 h 43 min

   = _____ h _____ min − _____ h _____ min

   = _____ h _____ min

   e.   23 h 20 min − 8 h 48 min

   = _____ h _____ min − _____ h _____ min

   = _____ h _____ min

   f.   10 h 25 min − 3 h 55 min

   = _____ h _____ min − _____ h _____ min

   = _____ h _____ min

   g.   16 h 19 min − 2 h 42 min

   = _____ h _____ min − _____ h _____ min

   = _____ h _____ min

Lesson 16.5   Elapsed Time

Fill in the boxes with the correct time.
Then draw the hands on the clock.

1.

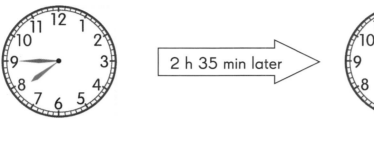

7:45 P.M.

2 h 35 min later

2.

50 min before

2:15 P.M.

Find the elapsed time. Draw a timeline to help you.

Example

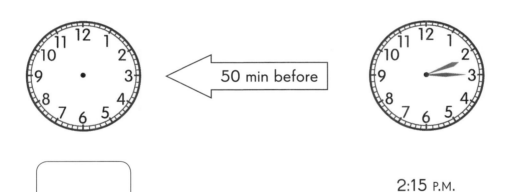

8:35 A.M. to 10:20 A.M.   <u>1h 45 min</u>

25 min   1 h   20 min

8:35 A.M.   9:00 A.M.   10:00 A.M.   10:20 A.M.

25 min + 1 h + 20 min = 1 h 45 min

3.   5:40 P.M. to 8:10 P.M. _____.

4.   10:50 A.M. to 2:30 P.M. _____.

Solve. Draw a timeline to help you.

5.   Mason took 2 hours 35 minutes to repair the fence in his garden.
He finishes repairing it at 4:25 P.M.
When did Mason start repairing the fence?

6. A supermarket opens at 7:30 A.M.
It stays open for 14 hours 30 minutes each day.
At what time does the supermarket close?

7. Class 3 students go to the Zoo for Learning Journey from
8:45 A.M. to 2:30 P.M.
How long is their learning journey?

8.   Chantel and her family took a bus from home to the library. They left home at 9:30 A.M. and reached the library at 12 P.M. How long did the trip to the library take?

9.   Tom fell asleep at 10:45 P.M. He woke up when the alarm clock went off at 6:30 A.M. How long did Tom sleep?

Lesson 16.6   Measuring Temperature

Write each temperature using °F.
Then write *hot*, *warm*, *cool*, or *cold* to describe the temperature.

1.

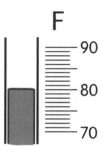

_____ °F

_____

2.

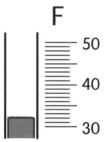

_____

_____

3.

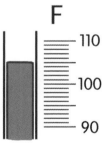

_____

_____

4.

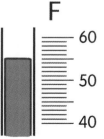

_____

_____

5.

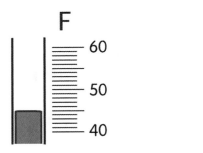

_____

_____

6.

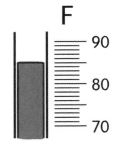

_____

_____

7.

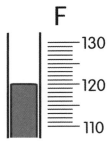

_____

_____

8.

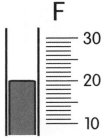

_____

_____

Solve.

9. Write the temperatures in order, from coldest to warmest.

96°F   69°F   76°F

_____

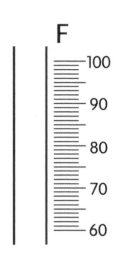

10. Write the temperatures in order, from warmest to coldest.

64°F   46°F   52°F

_____

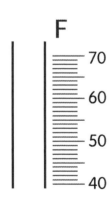

Decide which activity matches the temperature.

11. Are people ice skating on a pond or swimming in a pool?

_____

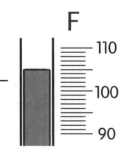

Decide which temperature matches the activity.

12.   Jimmy and his classmates are playing soccer at a field. Would the temperature be 68°F or 120°F?

_____

Complete.

13.   The temperature outside is 50°F.
The temperature in a classroom is 72°F.
How much warmer is the classroom?

14.   Water boils at _____°F.

15.   Water freezes at _____°F.

Lesson 16.7   Real-World Problems: Time and Temperature

Solve.

1. Linda looks after her baby sister for 3 hours 25 minutes when her mother goes shopping.
How many minutes does Linda look after her baby sister?

2. Karen started making a cake for her brother at 1:30 P.M. She took the cake out of the oven at 4:10 P.M.
How long did it take Karen to make the cake?

3. Matthew leaves home at 11:40 A.M. and arrives at the school at 12:15 P.M. How many minutes does it take for Matthew to get to school?

4. A boat ride starts at 12:45 P.M. and returns at 2:10 P.M. How long is the boat ride?

5. Marian practices ballet for 1 hour 30 minutes in the morning
and 45 minutes in the afternoon.
How long does Marian practice ballet in all?
Give your answer in hours and minutes.

6. Mr. Cruise travels 2 hours 40 minutes from Town P to Town Q.
He travels 1 hour 55 minutes from Town Q to Town R.
How long does he travel altogether?

7.   Richard took 2 hours 25 minutes to bake some muffins.
Then he took 3 hours 48 minutes to bake some rolls.
How much time did Richard spend baking the muffins and the rolls?

8.   Peggy takes 1 hour 25 minutes to prepare her family dinner.
Gary takes 2 hours 40 minutes to prepare his family dinner.
How much longer does it take Gary to prepare dinner than Peggy?

9.   A school choir practices for 1 hour 45 minutes on Friday and 3 hours on Saturday.
How much shorter than the Friday practice is the Saturday practice?

10.   Madeline is away from home for 3 hours 10 minutes to watch a show. Her sister, Rosie, is away from home for 1 hour 55 minutes to go shopping. Both of them leave home at the same time. How much earlier does Rosie return home?

11.   The temperature at noon is 80°F.
Late evening, the temperature is 52°F.
What is the difference between the two temperatures during that day?

12.   The recipe for a pizza says to preheat the oven to 450°F before putting
the pizza in the oven.
The oven temperature is now 365°F. How much hotter should the oven
get before you put in the pizza?

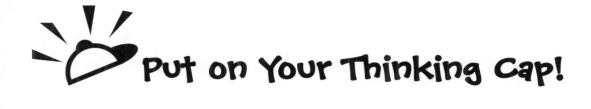

Put on Your Thinking Cap!

1. When Joanne wakes up, the clock shows 6:15 A.M.
It takes her 15 minutes to get dressed, 18 minutes to have breakfast
and 25 minutes to travel to school.
School starts at 7:20 A.M. Will Joanne arrive at school on time?

2. Six planes leave the airport at equal intervals.
The first plane leaves at 8:45 A.M. and the last plane leaves at 10:15 A.M.
At what time does the third plane leave?

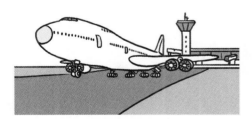

3.   The doctor gives Amanda ointment for her wound.
Amanda needs to apply the ointment every 40 minutes, eight times per day.
Amanda first applies the ointment at 2:50 P.M. At what time will she apply
the ointment for the last time that day?

4. Kanye's birthday is in March.
- This year, his birthday is not on a weekend.
- The date has two digits.
- You say the date when you count by twos.
- The sum of the two digits is 9.

MARCH

Sun	Mon	Tue	Wed	Thu	Fri	Sat
	1	2	3	4	5	6
7	8	9	10	11	12	13
14	15	16	17	18	19	20
21	22	23	24	25	26	27
28	29	30	31			

What is the date of Kanye's birthday?

5. Today is Monday, August 7th.
There are 31 days in August.
Marina's birthday is on September 6th.
On what day of the week is Marina's birthday?
Write the steps you followed to answer the question.

Angles and Lines

Lesson 17.1   Understanding and Identifying Angles

Check (✓) if an angle is shown.

1.

2.

3.

4.

5.

6.

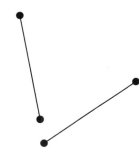

Mark two angles in each shape and object.

7.

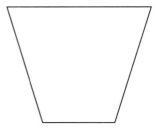

8.

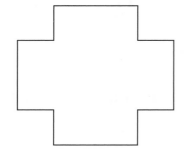

9.

10.

11.

12.

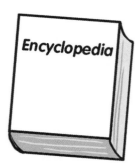

Lesson 17.2   Right Angles

Classify the angles and fill in the table.

Use **to help you.**

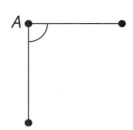

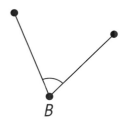

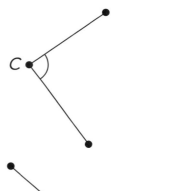

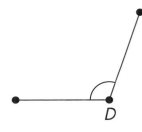

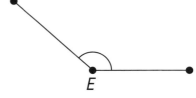

1.

Smaller than a Right Angle	Right Angle	Larger than a Right Angle

Mark all the right angles in each letter and number.

2.
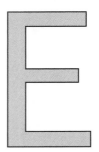

3.
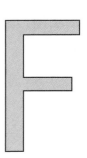

4.
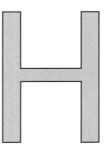

5.
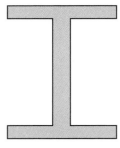

6.
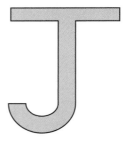

7.
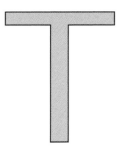

8.
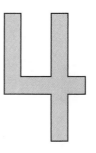

9.

Lesson 17.3　Perpendicular Lines

Name the perpendicular line segments in each figure.

Use a piece of folded paper **to help you.**

1.

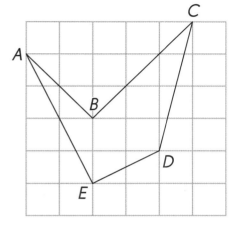

Segments _____ and _____

Segments _____ and _____

2.

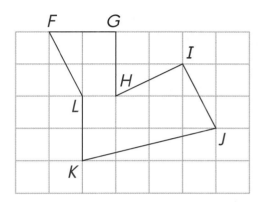

Segments _____ and _____

Segments _____ and _____

3.

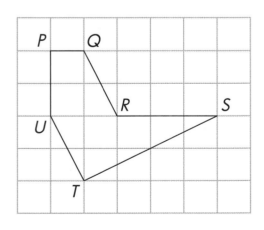

Segments _____ and _____

Segments _____ and _____

4.

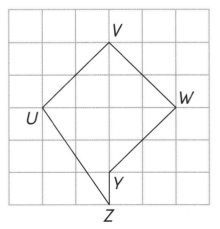

Segments _____ and _____

Segments _____ and _____

Name: _____ Date: _____

Name the perpendicular line segments in each figure.

Use a piece of folded paper to help you.

5.

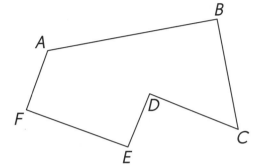

_____

_____

_____

6.

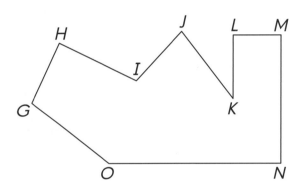

_____

_____

_____

7.

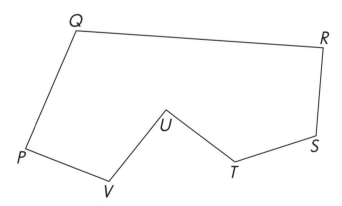

_____

_____

Lesson 17.4   Parallel Lines

Use a colored pencil to trace a pair of parallel lines or line segments.

1.

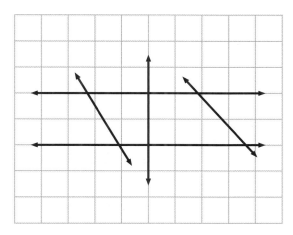

2.

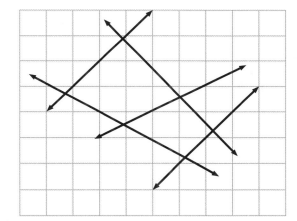

3.

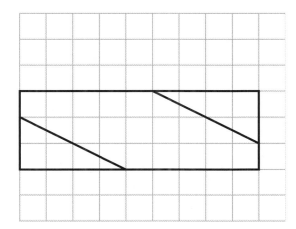

Name the pairs of parallel line segments in each figure.

4.

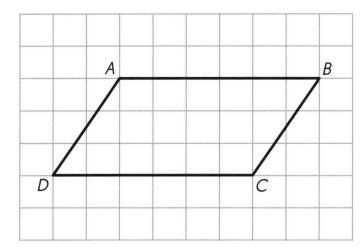

_____

_____

5.

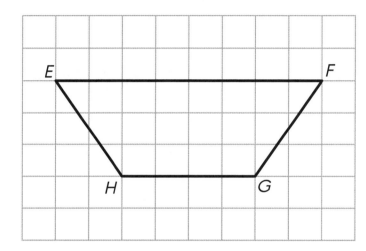

_____

6.

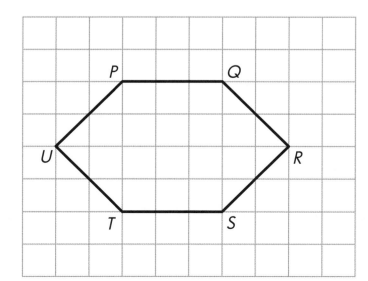

_____

_____

 **Put on Your Thinking Cap!**

Complete.

1.

Shape	Number of Sides	Number of Angles	Number of Right Angles
(right triangle)			
(square)			
(parallelogram)			
(pentagon)			
(hexagon)			
(cross/irregular shape)			

Draw each figure on grid paper.

2. A 3-sided figure
with 1 right angle

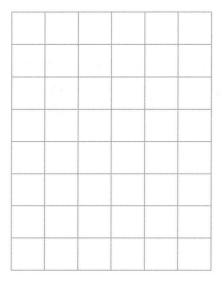

3. A 4-sided figure
with 2 right angles

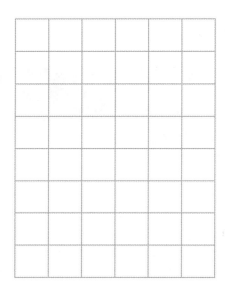

4. A 4-sided figure
with 4 right angles

5. A 6-sided figure
with 3 right angles

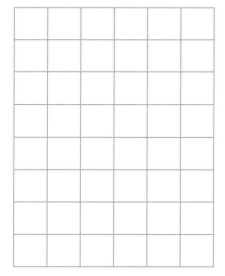

CHAPTER 18 Two-Dimensional Shapes

Lesson 18.1   Classifying Polygons

Identify each polygon. Use the words in the box.

| triangle | parallelogram | rectangle | square | octagon |
| rhombus | trapezoid | pentagon | hexagon | |

1.

_____

2.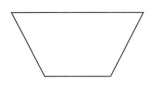

_____

3.

_____

4.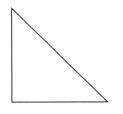

_____

5.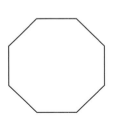

_____

6.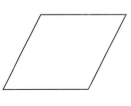

_____

7.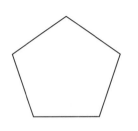

_____

8.

_____

9.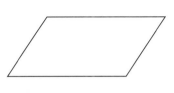

_____

Mark the angles of each polygon. Then complete the table.

10.

Polygon	Number of Sides	Number of Vertices	Number of Angles
triangle			
square			
pentagon			
hexagon			
octagon			

Name: _____ **Date:** _____

Are these statements correct? Write *true* or *false*.

11. All polygons have four sides. _____

12. A pentagon has four sides, four angles, and four vertices. _____

13. An octagon has eight vertices, eight sides, and eight angles. _____

14. Both rectangles and squares have four right angles each. _____

15. A trapezoid can have two right angles. _____

16. A parallelogram can be separated into two triangles. _____

Identify each quadrilateral. Then explain your answer.

17.

This is a _____

_____

_____

_____

18.

This is a _____

_____

_____

_____

19.

This is a _____

_____

_____

_____

Solve.

20.   How is a rhombus different from a parallelogram?

_____

_____

_____

_____

21.   How is a trapezoid similar to a parallelogram?

_____

_____

_____

_____

Are these statements corrected? Write *true* or *false*.

22.   A square has four right angles. _____

23.   A rectangle may or may not be a square. _____

24.   A quadrilateral has five angles. _____

25.   A parallelogram is not always a square. _____

26.   A rhombus has two pairs of parallel sides, four sides that are of equal length,

and four angles. _____

27.   Sometimes, a trapezoid has two right angles. _____

Lesson 18.2 Congruent Figures

Trace one of the two figures.
Cut out the traced figure and place it on top of the other figure.
Are the figures congruent? Write *yes* or *no*.

1.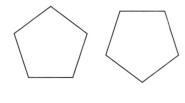

_____

2.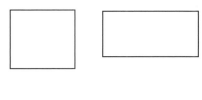

_____

3.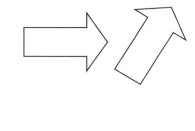

_____

4.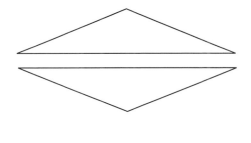

_____

5.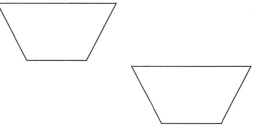

_____

6.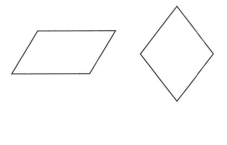

_____

7.   Draw a congruent figure. Trace the shape. Cut it out and draw a congruent figure by sliding it from left to right.

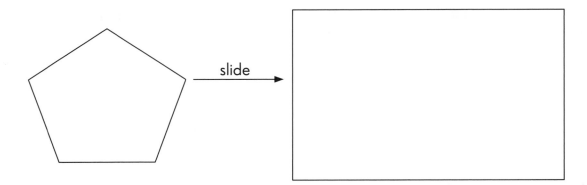

8.   Circle the figure that shows a flip.

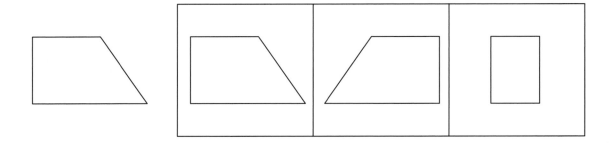

9.   Circle the figure that shows a turn.

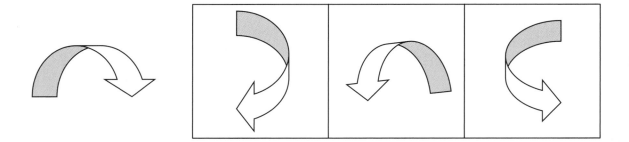

Lesson 18.3 Symmetry

**Decide whether the figures are symmetric. Write *yes* or *no*.
If the figure is symmetric, color half of the figure.**

1.

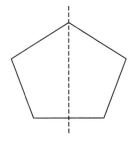

_____

2.

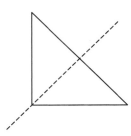

_____

3.

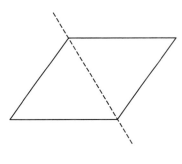

_____

4.

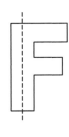

_____

5.

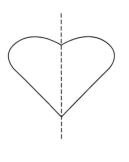

_____

6.

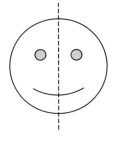

_____

7.

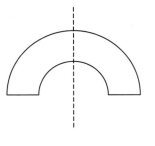

_____

8.

_____

Name: _____ Date: _____

Decide whether the dotted line is a line of symmetry. Write *yes* or *no*.

9.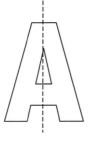

_____

10.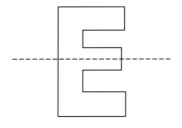

_____

11.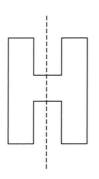

_____

12.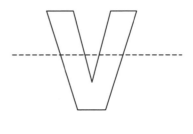

_____

13.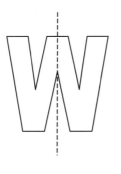

_____

14.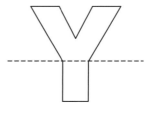

_____.

Name: _____   **Date:** _____

 Put on Your Thinking Cap!

Cut out the tangram below and use the pieces to form shapes.
Use combinations of 2, 3, 4, 5, 6, or 7 pieces for each shape.
Complete the chart by checking the box for the number of pieces used.

Shape	Number of Pieces Used						
	1	**2**	**3**	**4**	**5**	**6**	**7**
Square							
Triangle							
Rectangle							
Parallelogram							
Trapezoid							

- -

Tangram

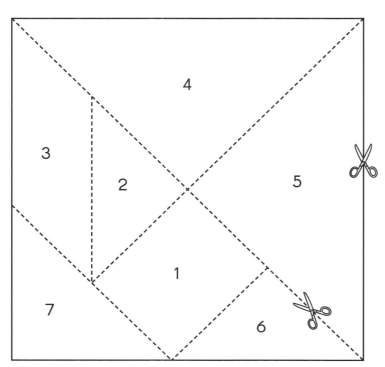

BLANK

CHAPTER 19 Area and Perimeter

Lesson 19.1   Area

1.   Draw and color two different figures on the grid.
     Use 5 squares (☐) and 4 half-squares (◺) for each figure.

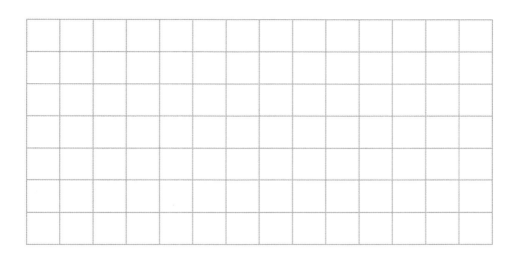

**In the figures, each square is 1 square unit and each half-square
is $\frac{1}{2}$ square unit. Find the area of each figure.**

2.

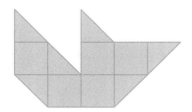

Area = _____ square units

3.

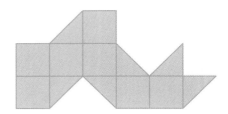

Area = _____ square units

4.

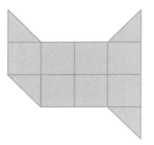

Area = _____ square units

5.

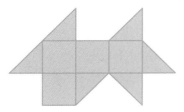

Area = _____ square units

6.

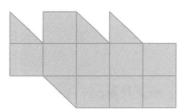

Area = _____ square units

7.

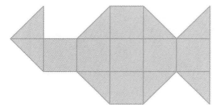

Area = _____ square units

Lesson 19.2   Square Units (cm² and in.²)

Find the area of each shaded figure.

1.

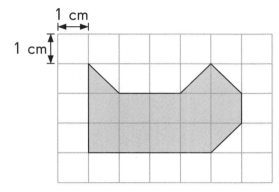

Area = _____ cm²

2.

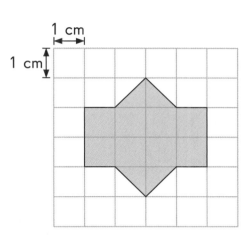

Area = _____ cm²

3.

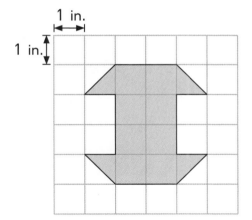

Area = _____ in.²

4.

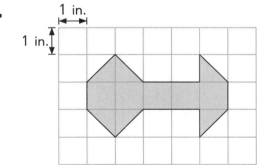

Area = _____ in.²

These inch squares are smaller than in real life.

Draw each figure on the grid.

5. A figure of area 6 cm²

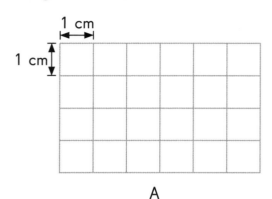

A

6. A figure of area 10 cm²

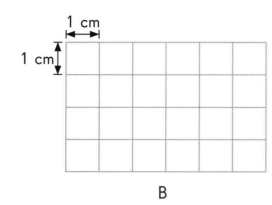

B

7. Which figure has the larger area? Figure _____

8. How can you make both figures have the same area?

_____

_____

9. A figure of area 10 in.²

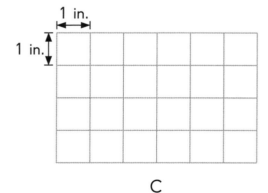

C

10. A figure of area 12 in.²

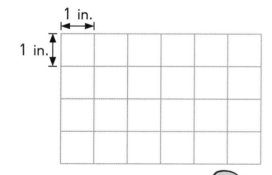

D

11. Which figure has the smaller area? Figure _____

12. How can you make both figures have the same area?

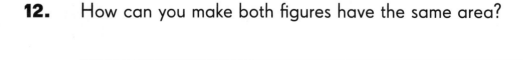

_____

_____

These inch squares are smaller than in real life.

Name: _____   Date: _____

Lesson 19.3   Square Units (m² and ft²)

Find the area of each figure in square meters.

1.

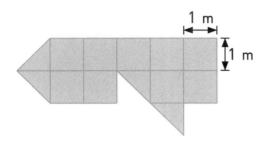

Area = _____ m²

2.

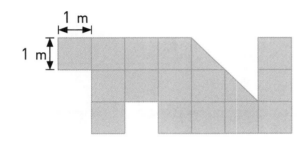

Area = _____ m²

Find the area of each figure in square feet.

3.

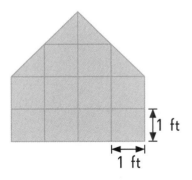

Area = _____ ft²

4.

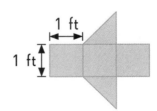

Area = _____ ft²

Use a meterstick and tape to make a square piece of paper with an area of 1 square meter.
Then use it to estimate the area of the following.

5.   About how many square meters would cover your closet door?

_____ m²

6.   About how many square meters would cover the top of your bed?

_____ m²

7.   List two objects at home that have an area less than
           1 square meter.

a. _____   **b.** _____

Use an inch ruler and tape to make a square piece of paper with an area of 1 square foot.
Then use it to estimate the area of the following.

8.   About how many square feet would cover your dining table?

_____ ft²

9.   About how many square feet would cover your door?

_____ ft²

10.   List two objects at home that have an area greater
           than 1 square foot.

a. _____   **b.** _____

Lesson 19.4   Perimeter and Area

Find the perimeter and area of each shaded figure.

1.

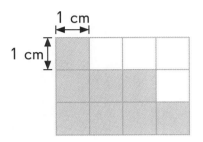

Perimeter = _____ cm

Area = _____ cm²

2.

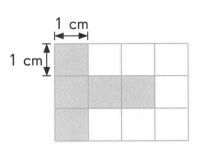

Perimeter = _____ cm

Area = _____ cm²

Find the perimeter and area of each shaded figure.

3.

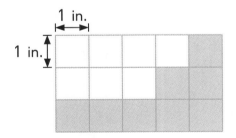

Perimeter = _____ in.

Area = _____ in.²

4.

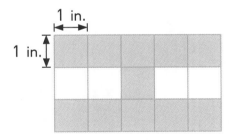

Perimeter = _____ in.

Area = _____ in.²

These inch squares are smaller than in real life.

Find the perimeter and area of each shaded figure.

5.

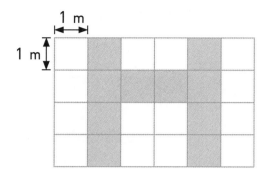

Perimeter = _____ m

Area = _____ m²

6.

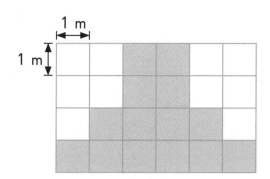

Perimeter = _____ m

Area = _____ m²

Find the perimeter and area of each shaded figure.

7.

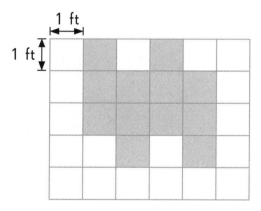

Perimeter = _____ ft

Area = _____ ft²

8.

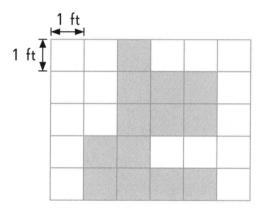

Perimeter = _____ ft

Area = _____ ft²

9. Draw and color two different figures each with a perimeter of 12 centimeters.

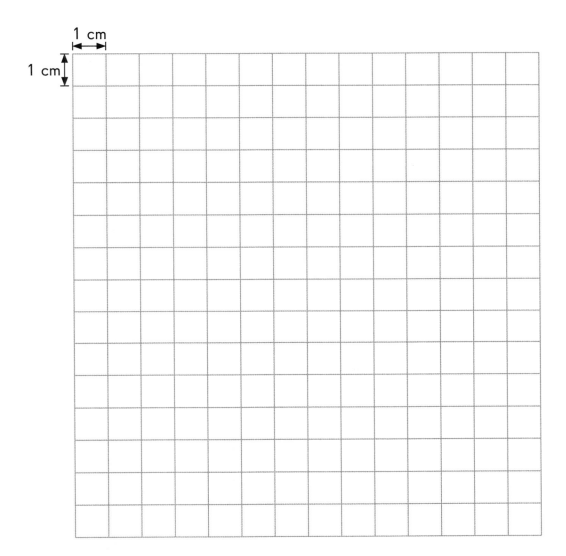

Do they have the same area? _____

10.   Draw and color two different figures each with an area
of 5 square inches.

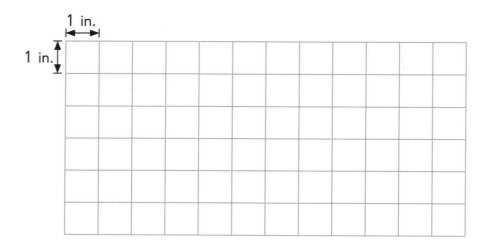

Do they have the same perimeter?_____

These inch squares are
smaller than in real life.

Lesson 19.5   More Perimeter

Find the perimeter of each figure.

1.

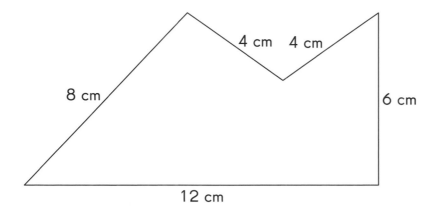

Perimeter = _____ + _____ + _____ + _____ + _____

= _____ cm

2.

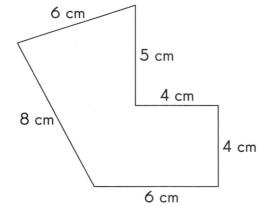

Perimeter = _____ + _____ + _____ + _____ + _____ + _____

= _____ cm

3.

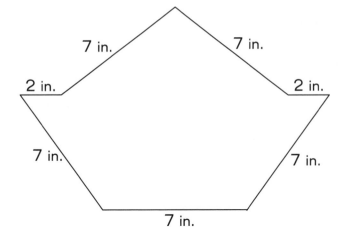

Perimeter = ___ + ___ + ___ + ___ + ___ + ___ + ___

= ___ in.

4.

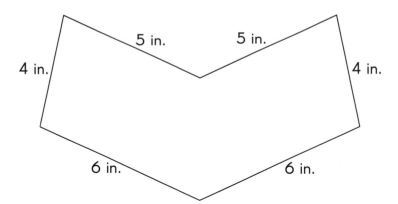

Perimeter = ___ + ___ + ___ + ___ + ___ + ___

= ___ in.

Find the perimeter of each figure.

5.

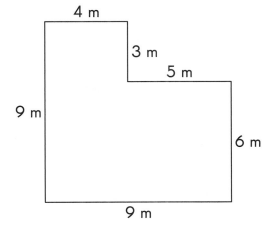

Perimeter = _____ m

6.

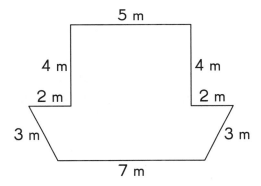

Perimeter = _____ m

7.

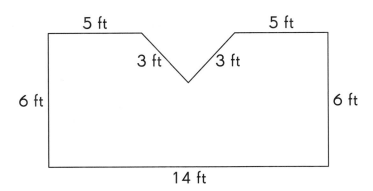

Perimeter = _____ ft

8. Each student in a group glued a ribbon around a square card that has a side of 15 centimeters. There are 3 students in the group. What was the total length of ribbon they used?

9. Three square tables are arranged next to each other to form one large rectangular table. The perimeter of the large rectangular table in 24 meters.
What is the perimeter of each square table?

Tables

Put on Your Thinking Cap!

Mason uses square tiles to form a series of squares as shown.

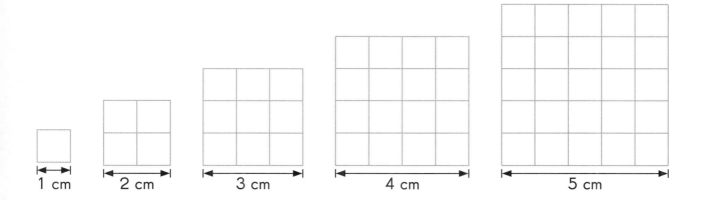

1 cm   2 cm   3 cm   4 cm   5 cm

1.   Find the perimeter and area of each square and complete the table.

Side Length (cm)	Perimeter (cm)	Area (cm²)
1	4	1
2	8	4
3		
4		
5		

2.   The smallest perimeter is _____ centimeters.

3.   The largest area is _____ square centimeters.

Four rectangular tiles can be used to make two different rectangles as shown.

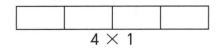 or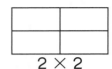

4. How many different rectangles can you make from twelve rectangular tiles? Draw the figures in the space below.

5. The figure below is made up of five squares of side 8 cm. Find the perimeter of the figure.

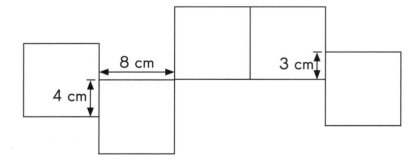

Name: _____ **Date:** _____

End-of-Year Test Prep

100

Multiple Choice (20 × 2 points = 40 points)

Fill in the circle next to the correct answer.

1. Tara and her brother are making a snowman.
What is the temperature outdoors?

(A) 30°F   (B) 60°F   (C) 68°F   (D) 105°F

2. How many tens are there in the quotient of 780 ÷ 3?

(A) 16   (B) 26   (C) 160   (D) 260

3. Complete the number pattern.

| 1 | 4 | 9 | 16 | 25 | _____ |

(A) 30   (B) 35   (C) 36   (D) 38

4. What number belongs in the 'start' circle?

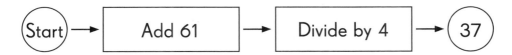

(A) 37   (B) 70   (C) 87   (D) 209

5.  +  = 252

 +  = 153

 = ?

(A) 18   (B) 28   (C) 38   (D) 48

6. Use each digit once to form the least 4-digit odd number.

8   2   3   0

(A) 2,083   (B) 2,308   (C) 2,038   (D) 3,546

7. The area of the figure is _____ square inches.

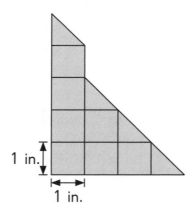

1 in.

1 in.

(A) 7   (B) 9   (C) 10   (D) 11

8. How many right angles are in the plane shape?

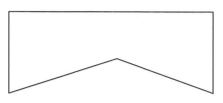

(A) 1   (B) 2   (C) 3   (D) 5

9. The perimeter of the mat is _____ feet.

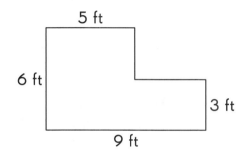

(A) 23   (B) 26   (C) 30   (D) 32

10. Mother buys 1 gallon of orange juice. She drinks 2 cups of orange juice every morning. How much orange juice is left after one week?

(A) 1 cup   (B) 1 quart   (C) 2 pints   (D) 1 pint

11. What fraction of the squares are shaded?

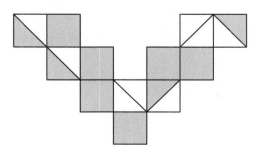

(A) $\frac{2}{3}$ (B) $\frac{5}{6}$ (C) $\frac{1}{2}$ (D) $\frac{1}{3}$

12. Alex buys a cake for $18.90 and some pies.
He gives the cashier two $20 bills and gets $6.50 in change.
How much does Alex pay for the pies?

(A) $14.60   (B) $21.10   (C) $23.50   (D) $25.40

13. Mrs. Gomez bakes a cake. Lily eats $\frac{3}{10}$ of the cake. Brian eats $\frac{1}{10}$ of the cake. How much of the cake is left?

Choose the answer that is in its simplest form.

(A) $\frac{1}{10}$ (B) $\frac{3}{5}$ (C) $\frac{2}{5}$ (D) $\frac{7}{10}$

14. Marina has 3 kilograms 50 grams of flour. She uses 760 grams of flour. How much flour does Marina have left?

(A) 410 g   (B) 1,110 g   (C) 2,290 g   (D) 2,740 g

15. Alan leaves his house and goes to the community club to play basketball. Then, he goes to a food court for dinner. How far has Alan traveled?

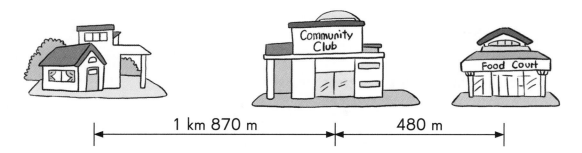

1 km 870 m   480 m

(A) 2,350 m   (B) 2,700 m   (C) 4,500 m   (D) 4,700 m

16. What is the volume of water in the container?

(A) 500 mL   (B) 520 mL   (C) 600 mL   (D) 700 mL

17.

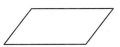

Which figure is congruent to the above figure?

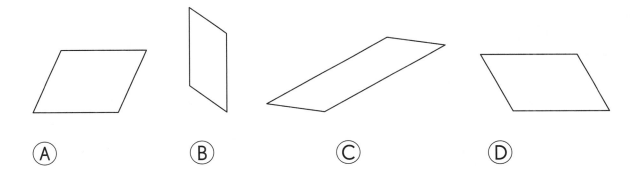

(A)   (B)   (C)   (D)

18. Two loaves of bread weigh 32 ounces. A pumpkin weighs 3 pounds. How much do the two loaves of bread and the pumpkin weigh in all?

(A) 1 pound   (B) 4 pounds

(C) 5 pounds   (D) 80 pounds

19. Sean spends 4 hours 40 minutes in school on Monday.
He spends 3 hours 45 minutes in school on Tuesday.
How much time does Sean spend in school on the two days?

(A) 8 h 25 min   (B) 7 h 25 min

(C) 7 h 5 min   (D) 55 min

20. Which line shows a line of symmetry?

(A) 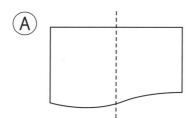   (B)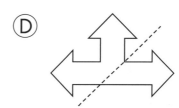

(C)   (D)

Short Answer (20 × 2 points = 40 points)

Write the correct answer in the space provided.

21. Shade 72°F on the thermometer.

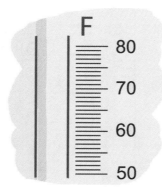

Name: _____ **Date:** _____

22. Complete each number pattern.

    a.   400, 300, 340, 240, 280, _____, _____

    b.   2, 2, 6, 30, _____, 1,890

23. What is the mass of the duck?

_____ kg _____ g

24. There are _____ angles in a pentagon.

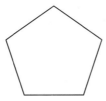

25. Find the missing numerator and denominator.

    a. $\dfrac{3}{4} = \dfrac{\Box}{8}$ **a.** _____

    b. $\dfrac{2}{5} = \dfrac{4}{\Box}$ **b.** _____

26. Order the fractions from greatest to least.

$$\frac{3}{4} \qquad \frac{7}{12} \qquad \frac{2}{3}$$

_____

27. What fraction of the shapes are triangles?

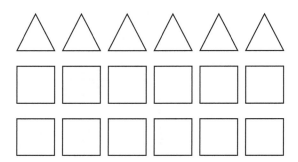

_____

28. Name a pair of perpendicular line segments in the figure.

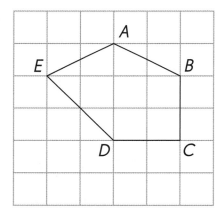

Segments _____ and _____

29. The length of a mat is 108 centimeters and its width is
65 centimeters. What is the perimeter of the mat?

_____ cm

30. Draw one or two dotted lines to break apart the trapezoid
into smaller polygons. Then list the polygons that you formed.

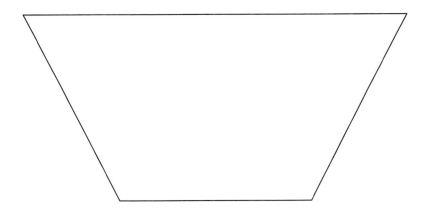

_____

_____

31.   What is the duration of time between 11:50 A.M. and 2:30 P.M.?

_____ h _____ min

32.   A concert starts at 7:45 P.M.
It lasts for 1 hour 50 minutes.
What time does the concert end?

_____

33.   Each toothpick is 2 inches long. Robert uses some toothpicks
to make this figure. What is the perimeter of the figure?

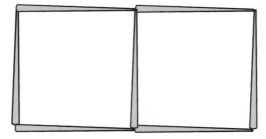

_____ in.

34. Name a pair of parallel line segments in the figure.

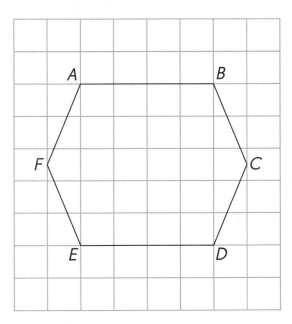

Segments _____ and _____

35. There is some mango juice in a jug. Lena pours all of it equally
into 7 glasses. Each glass contains 300 milliliters of mango juice.
How much mango juice did the jug have at first?

_____ L _____ mL

The bar graph shows the number of loaves of bread a bakery sells. Use the bar graph to answer Exercises 36 to 38.

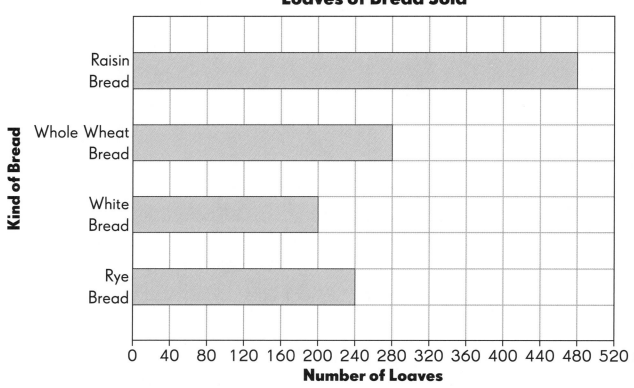

Loaves of Bread Sold

36. How many fewer loaves of white bread than whole wheat bread are sold?

_____

37. If the bakery made 300 loaves of rye bread, how many loaves of rye bread are not sold?

_____

38. Find the difference between the greatest number of loaves sold and the least number of loaves sold.

_____

The line plot shows the number of children in each family in a neighborhood. Use the line plot to answer Exercises 39 and 40.

Each ✗ represents one family.

Number of Children

39. How many families have fewer than two children?

_____

40. How many families live in this neighborhood?

_____

Extended Response (5 × 4 points = 20 points)

Solve. Show your work.

41. Box A has a mass of 1 kilogram 840 grams. Box B is 595 grams lighter than Box A. Find the mass of Box B.

42. Grandma Li gives some money equally to each of her 6 grandchildren. Each child gets $50 and Grandma Li has $160 left. Find the amount of money Grandma Li had to start with.

43. The distance between Point A and Point B is 5 kilometers 60 meters.
The distance between Point B and Point C is 1 kilometer 680 meters
shorter than the distance between Point A and Point B.
Find the distance between Point A and Point C.
Give your answer in kilometers and meters.

44. Kate goes to school on Saturdays. She spends 3 hours 35 minutes in school. She reaches home at 1:20 P.M. What time does Kate go to school?

45. Jeron has 30 coins. He has only dimes and quarters.
The total amount is $4.20. How many quarters does Jeron have?

Answers

Chapter 10

Lesson 10.1

1. $12 + $26 = $38
    25¢ + 55¢ = 80¢
    $38 + 80¢ = $38.80
    $12.25 + $26.55 = $38.80

2. $24 + $35 = $59
    5¢ + 75¢ = 80¢
    $59 + 80¢ = $59.80
    $24.05 + $35.75 = $59.80

3. $30.85   4. $2.80

5. $47.85   6. $16.00

7. $79.00   8. $10.30

9. $79.40

10. (80¢ / 20¢) — $1

    $17.35 + $1 = $18.35
    $18.35 − 20¢ = $18.15
    So, $17.35 + $0.80 = $18.15

11. (85¢ / 15¢) — $1

    $26.70 + $1 = $27.70
    $27.70 − 15¢ = $27.55
    So, $26.70 + $0.85 = $27.55

12. (75¢ / 25¢) — $1

    $34.45 + $1 = $35.45
    $35.45 − 25¢ = $35.20
    So, $34.45 + $0.75 = $35.20

13. (90¢ / 10¢) — $1

    $48.50 + $1 = $49.50
    $49.50 − 10¢ = $49.40
    So, $48.50 + $0.90 = $49.40

14. $7.95   15. $9.98

16. $69.95   17. $19.75

18. $39.70   19. $57.00

20. $90.35   21. $50.50

22. $4.35 + $6.75 = $11.10

23. $15.55 + $3.90 = $19.45

24. $1.65 + $1.65 + $6.75 = $10.05

25. $2.50 + $29.50 + $29.50 = $61.50

Lesson 10.2

1. $15 − $9 = $6
    85¢ − 30¢ = 55¢
    $6 + 55¢ = $6.55
    $15.85 − $9.30 = $6.55

2. $48 − $24 = $24
    65¢ − 45¢ = 20¢
    $24 + 20¢ = $24.20
    $48.65 − $24.45 = $24.20

3. $66 − $45 = $21
    80¢ − 30¢ = 50¢
    $21 + 50¢ = $21.50
    $66.80 − $45.30 = $21.50

4. $4.65   5. $28.40

6. $31.70   7. $9.05

8. $62.70

9. (85¢ / 15¢) — $1

    $12.30 − $1 = $11.30
    $11.30 + 15¢ = $11.45
    So, $12.30 − $0.85 = $11.45

10. (95¢ / 5¢) — $1

    $20.50 − $1 = $19.50
    $19.50 + 5¢ = $19.55
    So, $20.50 − $0.95 = $19.55

11. ($1.90 / 10¢) — $2

    $15.20 − $2 = $13.20
    $13.20 + 10¢ = $13.30
    So, $15.20 − $1.90 = $13.30

12. ($2.80 / 20¢) — $3

    $18.40 − $3 = $15.40
    $15.40 + 20¢ = $15.60
    So, $18.40 − $2.80 = $15.60

13. $1.63   14. $3.56

15. $24.62   16. $25.30

17. $14.06   18. $21.83

19. $63.45   20. $41.80

21. $5.05   22. $7.55

23. $10.20   24. $14.10

Lesson 10.3

1.

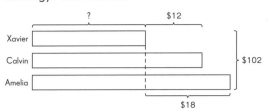

Matthew — $52, $7.15

Raja — ?

$52 + $7.15 = $59.15
Raja pays $59.15 for his pair of glasses.

2.

$100

$76.90   ?

$100 − $76.90 = $23.10
Mr. Larry receives $23.10.

3.

$28.60 $19.80

Emily

Emily's sister   b. ?

a. ?

a. $28.60 + $19.80 = $48.40
   Emily's sister saves $48.40.
b. $28.60 + $48.40 = $77.
   Both of them save $77.

4.

a. ?

$17.50 $24.90   b. ?

Lily   Zachary

$60

a. $17.50 + $24.90 = $42.40
   They have $42.40 altogether.
b. $60.00 − $42.40 = $17.60
   They must save $17.60 more to buy
   the present.

Put on Your Thinking Cap!

Thinking Skill: Analyzing parts and whole

1.

| $20 | $10 | $5 | $1 |
| 25¢ | 25¢ | 10¢ | 10¢ |

2.

$20	$20	$10
$5	$1	$1
25¢	10¢	

3. Thinking Skill: Comparing
    Strategy: Use a model

? $12

Xavier

Calvin $102

Amelia

$18

3 units → $102 − $12 − $18 = $72
1 unit → $72 ÷ 3 = $24
Xavier has $24.

4. Thinking Skill: Deduction
    Strategy: Guess and check

	Dimes	Quarters	Total number of coins	Amount	$3.80?
1st Guess	10	10	20	$3.50	No
2nd Guess	9	11	20	$3.65	No
3rd Guess	8	12	20	$3.80	Yes

There are 12 quarters in the piggy bank.

Chapter 11

Lesson 11.1

1. 680 cm
2. 543 cm
3. 806 cm
4. 1,235 cm
5. 1,507 cm
6. 2,812 cm
7. 1 m 85 cm
8. 3 m 12 cm
9. 7 m 8 cm
10. 9 m 36 cm
11. 12 m 3 cm
12. Eric — 143 cm
    Mary — 152 cm
    Ken — 160 cm
13. Ken
14. Lucy
15. 9 cm

Lesson 11.2

1. 8,000 m
2. 4,350 m
3. 7,900 m
4. 5,010 m
5. 2,095 m
6. 7,009 m
7. 3,005 m
8. 5 km

9. 6 km 340 m   10. 1 km 896 m
11. 2 km 65 m   12. 7 km 80 m
13. 4 km 2 m   14. 2 km 8 m
15. 3; 480   16. 8; 87
17. 5,750   18. 8,050
19. 9,005   20. 9,300
21. 7,700   22. 6; 450
23. 2; 200   24. ✓
25. ✓   26. ✗

Lesson 11.3

1. 900 g   2. 1 kg 300 g
3. 3 kg 800 g   4. 4 kg 200 g
5. 6,000 g   6. 3,438 g
7. 8,260 g   8. 2,370 g
9. 4,050 g   10. 5,090 g
11. 7,005 g   12. 9,008 g
13. 3 kg   14. 2 kg 850 g
15. 5 kg 643 g   16. 1 kg 865 g
17. 3 kg 80 g   18. 7 kg 55 g
19. 8 kg 5 g   20. 9 kg 18 g
21.

Less than 500 g	More than 500 g but less than 1 kg	From 1 kg to 1 kg 500 g	More than 1 kg 500 g
Cheese	Baked beans	Milk formula	Rice
Veggie chips	Peaches	Crabs	Detergent
Cereal	Cherries		

22. veggie chips   23. rice
24. 5   25. 2
26. 3,450 g; 2 kg 300 g; 1,280 g

Lesson 11.4

1. 80 mL   2. 350 mL
3. 600 mL   4. 200 mL
5. 2; 500   6. 1; 200
7. 3,250 mL   8. 4,600 mL
9. 2,080 mL   10. 6,070 mL
11. 1,009 mL   12. 5,006 mL
13. 1 L 800 mL   14. 2 L 130 mL
15. 3 L 550 mL   16. 4 L 90 mL

17. 6 L 0 mL   18. 5 L 8 mL
19.

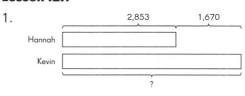

20. E
     C
     A
     B
     D
     F

21. equal to   22. more than
23. less than   24. less than
25. equal to   26. more than

Put on Your Thinking Cap!

Thinking skills: Comparing, Sequencing

1. 114   2. 226
3. B   4. D
5. 344   6. 3,316
7. park   8. Phoenix High School
9. 4,726

Chapter 12

Lesson 12.1

1.

	2,853	1,670
Hannah		
Kevin		
		?

2,853 + 1,670 = 4,523
4,523 m = 4,000 m + 523 m
        = 4 km 523 m
Kevin jogs 4 kilometers 523 meters.

2.

$90 \times 7 = 9 \text{ tens} \times 7$
$\qquad = 63 \text{ tens}$
$\qquad = 630$
$630 \text{ cm} = 600 \text{ cm} + 30 \text{ cm}$
$\qquad\qquad = 6 \text{ m } 30 \text{ cm}$
The total length of the string is 6 meters
30 centimeters.

3.

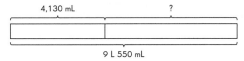

$207 \div 4 = 51 \text{ R } 3$
The maximum number of bricks the truck can
carry is 51.

4.

$9 \text{ L } 550 \text{ mL} = 9 \text{ L} + 550 \text{ mL}$
$\qquad\qquad\qquad = 9{,}000 \text{ mL} + 550 \text{ mL}$
$\qquad\qquad\qquad = 9{,}550 \text{ mL}$
$9{,}550 - 4{,}130 = 5{,}420$
$5{,}420 \text{ mL} = 5{,}000 \text{ mL} + 420 \text{ mL}$
$\qquad\qquad\quad = 5 \text{ L } 420 \text{ mL}$
5 liters 420 milliliters of water is needed to fill
the tank.

Lesson 12.2

1. $540 \div 4 = 135$
$135 \times 5 = 675$
Their total mass is 675 kilograms.

2.

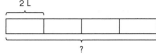

$4 \times 2 = 8$
$8 \text{ L} = 8{,}000 \text{ mL}$

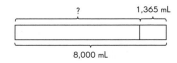

$8{,}000 - 1{,}365 = 6{,}635$
$6{,}635 \text{ mL} = 6{,}000 \text{ mL} + 635 \text{ mL}$
$\qquad\qquad\quad = 6 \text{ L } 635 \text{ mL}$
The chef uses 6 liters 635 milliliters of cooking oil.

3.

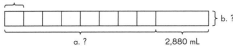

a. $100 \times 8 = 800$
There is 800 milliliters of medicine in the
8 bottles.
b. $800 + 2{,}880 = 3{,}680$
$3{,}680 \text{ mL} = 3{,}000 \text{ mL} + 680 \text{ mL}$
$\qquad\qquad\quad = 3 \text{ L } 680 \text{ mL}$
There is 3 liters 680 milliliters of medicine in all.

4.

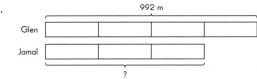

$992 \div 4 = 248$
$248 \times 3 = 744$
Jamal runs 744 meters.

5.

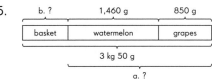

a. $1{,}460 + 850 = 2{,}310$
$2{,}310 \text{ g} = 2{,}000 \text{ g} + 310 \text{ g}$
$\qquad\qquad = 2 \text{ kg } 310 \text{ g}$
Total mass of the watermelon and the grapes
is 2 kilograms 310 grams.
b. $3 \text{ kg } 50 \text{ g} = 3 \text{ kg} + 50 \text{ g}$
$\qquad\qquad\qquad = 3{,}000 \text{ g} + 50 \text{ g}$
$\qquad\qquad\qquad = 3{,}050 \text{ g}$
$2 \text{ kg } 310 \text{ g} = 2 \text{ kg} + 310 \text{ g}$
$\qquad\qquad\qquad = 2{,}000 \text{ g} + 310 \text{ g}$
$\qquad\qquad\qquad = 2{,}310 \text{ g}$
$3{,}050 - 2{,}310 = 740$
The mass of the basket is 740 grams.

6.

$5 \text{ L } 330 \text{ mL} = 5 \text{ L} + 330 \text{ mL}$
$\qquad\qquad\qquad = 5{,}000 \text{ mL} + 330 \text{ mL}$
$\qquad\qquad\qquad = 5{,}330 \text{ mL}$
$5{,}330 - 850 = 4{,}480$
$2 \text{ units} \longrightarrow 4{,}480 \text{ mL}$
$1 \text{ unit} \longrightarrow 2{,}240 \text{ mL}$
The capacity of Jug B is 2,240 milliliters.

Put on Your Thinking Cap!

1. Thinking skill: Comparing
   Strategy: Use a model

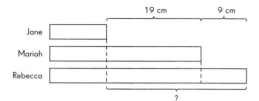

   $19 + 9 = 28$
   The difference in height between Jane and Rebecca is 28 centimeters.

2.

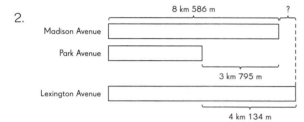

   a. $8,586 - 3,795 = 4,791$
      $4,791 \text{ m} = 4,000 \text{ m} + 791 \text{ m}$
      $\phantom{4,791 \text{ m}} = 4 \text{ km } 791 \text{ m}$
      Park Avenue is 4 kilometers 791 meters long.
   b. Lexington Avenue is longer.
      $4,134 - 3,795 = 339$
      Lexington Avenue is 339 meters longer than Madison Avenue.

Chapter 13

Lesson 13.1

1.

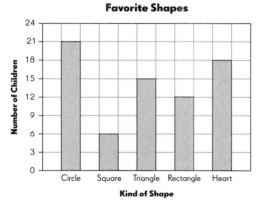

Favorite Shapes

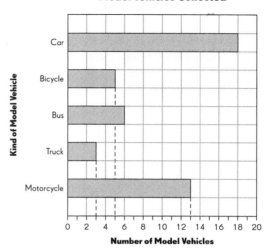

Model Vehicles Collected

Lesson 13.2

1.	12	2.	8
3.	34	4.	18
5.	80	6.	30
7.	strawberries	8.	12 children
9.	9 children	10.	oranges; grapes
11.	Answers vary.	12.	yellow
13.	33 students	14.	17
15.	blue; purple	16.	8,600 tourists
17.	The Grand Canyon	18.	Washington D.C.
19.	800	20.	Disneyland
21.	Statue of Liberty		

Lesson 13.3

1.

Number of Schools
6
3
10
5

2. Each **✗** stands for 1 school.

```
                    ✗
                    ✗
                    ✗
                    ✗
          ✗         ✗
          ✗         ✗   ✗
          ✗         ✗   ✗
          ✗   ✗     ✗   ✗
          ✗   ✗     ✗   ✗
          ✗   ✗     ✗   ✗
        ──────────────────→
          1   2     3   4
        Number of Gold Medals
```

3. 24 schools

4. 5 schools

5. 4 schools

6.
Number of Laps	Number of Children
2	12
3	6
4	8
5	4
6	2

7. Each ✗ stands for one child.

```
✗
✗
✗
✗
✗        ✗
✗        ✗
✗    ✗   ✗
✗    ✗   ✗
✗    ✗   ✗   ✗
✗    ✗   ✗   ✗
✗    ✗   ✗   ✗   ✗
✗    ✗   ✗   ✗   ✗
─────────────────────
2    3   4   5   6
   Number of Laps
```

8. 4 children

9. 14 children

10. 10 children

11. 32 children

12. Twice

13. 2;5 or 3;6

14. C

15. In line plot A, 5 students should have 9 points instead of 4 students.

16. In line plot B, 3 students should have 6 points instead of 2 students.

17. In line plot D, the least number on the number line should be 6 instead of 5. Also, the ✗s are misplaced. 4 students should have 7 points and 5 students should have 9 points.

18. A line plot of this data would be difficult to make and interpret, because the number of ✗s above each number on the number line would be very tall.

Put on Your Thinking Cap!

1. 6

2. Belita and Emily

3. Thinking skill: Comparing

Strategy: Solve part of the problem

Solution: $6 \times 3 = 18$

Anna has 3 times as many stamps as Belita.

4. Thinking skill: Comparing

Strategy: Solve part of the problem

Solution: $12 \div 2 = 6$

Belita has half as many stamps as Devon.

5. Thinking skill: Comparing

Strategy: Solve part of the problem

Solution: $18 + 9 = 27$

Yes, they will be able to collect 30 stamps.

6. Thinking skill: Comparing

Strategy: Solve part of the problem

Solution: $18 - 6 = 12$

The girl with the most stamps has 12 more stamps.

7. Thinking skill: Comparing

Strategy: Solve part of the problem

Solution:

a. $18 + 6 + 15 + 12 + 9 = 60$

$60 \div 5 = 12$

Each girl gets 12 stamps.

b. $18 - 12 = 6$

Anna would have to give away 6 stamps.

Chapter 14

Lesson 14.1

1. $\frac{4}{7}$; four; three

2. (e) $\frac{8}{8}$ (c) $\frac{3}{4}$

(r) $\frac{4}{5}$ (a) $\frac{5}{12}$

(s) $\frac{6}{8}$ (u) $\frac{1}{3}$

(q) $\frac{2}{6}$ (k) $\frac{7}{10}$

A box of quackers!

3. $\frac{2}{6}$ 4. $\frac{3}{8}$

5. $\frac{7}{12}$ 6. $\frac{4}{4}$

Lesson 14.2

1. $\frac{2}{12}$ 2. $\frac{2}{8}$

3. $\frac{2}{6}$ 4. $\frac{4}{8}$

5. $\frac{6}{8}$ 6. $\frac{4}{10}$

7. $\frac{8}{12}$ 8. $\frac{10}{12}$

9. $\frac{8}{10}$ 10. $\frac{9}{12}$

11. $\frac{4}{12}$ 12. $\frac{6}{9}$

13. Colour the mat as necessary to show the respective unit fractions.
14. These are equivalent fractions.
15. These are not equivalent fractions.
16. These are not equivalent fractions.
17. These are equivalent fractions.
18. These are equivalent fractions.
19. These are not equivalent fractions.
20. These are equivalent fractions.
21. These are equivalent fractions.

22. $\frac{2}{4} = \frac{3}{6} = \frac{6}{12}$

23. $\frac{9}{12}$ 24. $\frac{4}{6} = \frac{8}{12}$

25. $\frac{10}{12}$

Lesson 14.3

1. $\frac{6}{8}$ 2. $\frac{4}{10}$

3. $\frac{4}{12}$ 4. $\frac{9}{12}$

5. $\frac{10}{12}$ 6. $\frac{8}{10}$

7. $\frac{6}{12}$ 8. $\frac{6}{9}$

9. $\frac{4}{18}$

10. $\frac{6}{8} = \frac{9}{12} = \frac{12}{16}$

11. $\frac{6}{6} = \frac{9}{9} = \frac{12}{12}$

12. $\frac{6}{10} = \frac{9}{15} = \frac{12}{20}$

13. $\frac{4}{5}$

14. $\frac{3}{4}$ 15. $\frac{1}{3}$

16. $\frac{1}{2}$ 17. $\frac{3}{4}$

18. $\frac{1}{3}$ 19. $\frac{1}{2}$

20. $\frac{3}{5}$ 21. $\frac{4}{5}$

22. $\frac{1}{4}$ 23. $\frac{3}{4}$

24. $\frac{2}{3}$ 25. $\frac{5}{6}$

26. $\frac{1}{4}$ 27. $\frac{2}{5}$

28. $\frac{3}{4}$ 29. $\frac{2}{3}$

Lesson 14.4

1. $\frac{1}{2}; \frac{5}{7}$ 2. $\frac{7}{10}; \frac{1}{2}$

3. $\frac{2}{7}; \frac{5}{7}$ 4. $\frac{4}{6}; \frac{2}{6}$

5. $\frac{4}{7}; \frac{4}{5}$ 6. $\frac{3}{4}; \frac{3}{10}$

7. $\frac{8}{12}; \frac{7}{12} < \frac{2}{3}$ 8. $\frac{2}{8}; \frac{5}{8} > \frac{1}{4}$

9. $\frac{6}{9}; \frac{2}{9} < \frac{2}{3}$ 10. $<; >; <$

11. $\frac{2}{3}$ 12. $\frac{4}{5}$

13. $\frac{10}{11}$ 14. $\frac{4}{7}$

15. $\frac{1}{6}, \frac{1}{4}, \frac{1}{2}$ 16. $\frac{2}{3}, \frac{3}{4}, \frac{5}{6}$

17. $\frac{2}{6}, \frac{7}{12}, \frac{3}{4}$ 18. $\frac{5}{12}, \frac{5}{8}, \frac{5}{6}$

19. $\frac{3}{4}, \frac{1}{2}, \frac{3}{8}$ 20. $\frac{1}{3}, \frac{1}{6}, \frac{1}{9}$

21. $\frac{11}{12}, \frac{5}{6}, \frac{3}{4}$ 22. $\frac{2}{3}, \frac{2}{4}, \frac{2}{6}$

Lesson 14.5 (Part 1)

1. $\frac{3}{6}; \frac{4}{6}$ or $\frac{2}{3}$ 2. $\frac{6}{9}; \frac{7}{9}$

3. $\frac{4}{10}; \frac{5}{10}$ or $\frac{1}{2}$ 4. $\frac{5}{8}; \frac{8}{8}$ or 1

5. $\frac{2}{2}$ or 1 6. $\frac{3}{3}$ or 1

7. $\frac{3}{5}$ 8. $\frac{4}{6}$ or $\frac{2}{3}$

9. $\frac{2}{8}$ or $\frac{1}{4}$

$\frac{3}{8} + \frac{3}{8} = \frac{6}{8}$

$1 - \frac{6}{8} = \frac{8}{8} - \frac{6}{8} = \frac{2}{8}$ or $\frac{1}{4}$

10. $\frac{5}{10}$ or $\frac{1}{2}$

$\frac{2}{10} + \frac{3}{10} = \frac{5}{10}$

$1 - \frac{5}{10} = \frac{10}{10} - \frac{5}{10} = \frac{5}{10}$ or $\frac{1}{2}$

11. $\frac{3}{9}$ or $\frac{1}{3}$

$\frac{2}{9} + \frac{4}{9} = \frac{6}{9}$

$1 - \frac{6}{9} = \frac{9}{9} - \frac{6}{9} = \frac{3}{9}$ or $\frac{1}{3}$

Lesson 14.5 (Part 2)

1. $\frac{3}{6}$; $\frac{2}{6}$ or $\frac{1}{3}$ 2. $\frac{4}{12}$; $\frac{3}{12}$ or $\frac{1}{4}$

3. $\frac{3}{8}$; $\frac{4}{8}$ or $\frac{1}{2}$ 4. $\frac{3}{10}$; $\frac{6}{10}$ or $\frac{3}{5}$

5. $\frac{3}{8}$ 6. $\frac{4}{9}$

7. $\frac{2}{7}$ 8. $\frac{5}{11}$

9. $\frac{2}{6}$ or $\frac{1}{3}$ 10. $\frac{1}{12}$

11. $\frac{1}{4}$ 12. $\frac{1}{3}$

13. $\frac{5}{12}$

$\frac{8}{12} - \frac{1}{12} = \frac{7}{12}$

$1 - \frac{7}{12} = \frac{12}{12} - \frac{7}{12} = \frac{5}{12}$

Lesson 14.6

1. $\frac{1}{3}$ 2. $\frac{1}{4}$

3. $\frac{3}{5}$ 4. $\frac{3}{6}$

5. 1 unit ⟶ 12 ÷ 3 = 4
    2 units ⟶ 4 × 2 = 8
    $\frac{2}{3}$ of 12 is 8.

So, 8 of the beetles are brown.

6. 12
    4 units ⟶ 16
    1 unit ⟶ 16 ÷ 4 = 4
    3 units ⟶ 4 × 3 = 12

7. 15
    8 units ⟶ 24
    1 unit ⟶ 24 ÷ 8 = 3
    5 units ⟶ 3 × 5 = 15

8. 12
    7 units ⟶ 21
    1 unit ⟶ 21 ÷ 7 = 3
    4 units ⟶ 3 × 4 = 12

9. 40
    3 units ⟶ 60
    1 unit ⟶ 60 ÷ 3 = 20
    2 units ⟶ 20 × 2 = 40

Put on Your Thinking Cap!

1. Thinking skills: Comparing, Analyzing parts
    and whole
    Strategy: Use a model
    Solution:

$\frac{3}{8} + \frac{1}{4} = \frac{5}{8}$

$\frac{8}{8} - \frac{5}{8} = \frac{3}{8}$

$\frac{3}{8}$ liter of mango juice is left at the end of the second day.

2. Thinking skills: Analyzing parts and whole,
    Spatial visualization
    Strategy: Use a model

    a. $\frac{1}{4}$ b. $\frac{1}{2}$

    c. $\frac{1}{2}$ d. $\frac{1}{2}$

    e. $\frac{3}{4}$ f. $\frac{1}{2}$

3. Thinking skills: Comparing, Analyzing parts
and whole

Strategy: Use a model

Solution:

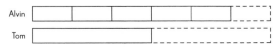

Box X

Box Y

$\frac{2}{9}$ of the sand from Box X must be poured into
Box Y.

4. Thinking skills: Comparing, Analyzing parts and
whole, Deduction

Strategy: Use a model

Solution:

Before

Alvin

Tom

Now

Alvin

Tom

?

Tom had $\frac{1}{2}$ or $\frac{3}{6}$ of a pizza at first.

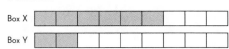

Chapter 15

Lesson 15.1

1. 3	2. 6
3. 3	4. 4
5. $5\frac{1}{2}$	6. $3\frac{1}{2}$
7. $1\frac{1}{2}$	8. 5
9. 3	10. 3
11. 4	12. 2
13. 12	14. 3; 36
15. a	16. a
17. b	18. b
19. 1	20. 20
21. 3	22. 40
23. feet or yards	24. inches
25. feet or yards	26. miles

Lesson 15.2

1. 25	2. 4
3. 8	4. 6
5. 2	6. 7
7. pounds	8. ounces
9. tons	10. ounces
11. pounds	12. tons
13. 4 oz, 8 lb, 2 T	14. 10 oz, 3 lb, 1 T
15. b	16. c
17. d	18. tons or pounds
19. ounces	20. pounds
21. tons or pounds	

Lesson 15.3

1. 10	2. 10
3. 4	4. 4
5. 6	6. 6
7. 18	8. 18
9. a	10. a

11.

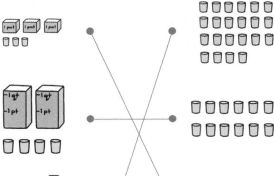

12. 6 pt,   1 gal,   8 qt

13. 2 qt,   8 pt,   20 c

14. 1 qt,   3 pt,   8 c

15. 3 pt,   2 qt,   1 gal

16. cups or pints

17. cups, pints, or quarts

18. gallons

Put on Your Thinking Cap!

1. Thinking skill: Comparing

   Strategy: Use a model

   Solution:

   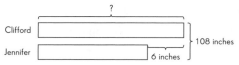

   108 in. − 6 in. = 102 in.
   102 in. ÷ 2 = 51 in.
   51 in. + 6 in. = 57 in.
   Clifford is 57 inches tall.

2. Thinking skill: Comparing

   Strategy: Use a model

   Solution:

   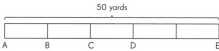

   5 units → 50 yd
    1 unit → 50 yd ÷ 5 = 10 yd
    2 units → 10 yd × 2 = 20 yd
   The distance between Tree D and Tree E is 20 yards.

3. Thinking skill: Comparing

   Strategy: Use a model

   Solution:

   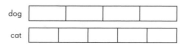

   Distance walked by the dog in 4 steps
   = 1 ft × 4 = 4 ft
   Distance walked by the cat in 5 steps
   = 4 ft
   (5 × 4 = 20)
   Distance walked by the cat in 20 steps
   = 4 ft × 4 = 16 ft
   The cat walks 16 feet when it takes 20 steps.

4. Thinking skill: Comparing

   Strategy: Make a systematic list

   Solution:

Number of Leaps	Rabbit (feet)	Kangaroo (feet)
0	120	0
1	125	15
2	130	30
3	135	45
4	140	60
5	145	75
6	150	90
7	155	105
8	160	120
9	165	135
10	170	150
11	175	165
12	180	180

The kangaroo makes 12 leaps to catch up to the rabbit.

Test Prep for Chapters 10 to 15

1. C
2. C
3. A
4. B
5. C
6. C
7. D
8. B
9. C
10. A
11. 64
12. $\frac{7}{12}, \frac{2}{3}, \frac{5}{6}$
13. 47 cm
14. 512 g
15. $\frac{7}{8}$
16. $\frac{5}{6}$
17. $20.75
18. 2,580
19. 32
20. $8.70
21. 5 L 60 mL = 5,000 mL + 60 mL
            = 5,060 mL
    5,060 mL − 1,850 mL = 3,210 mL
    3,210 mL = 3,000 mL + 210 mL
            = 3 L 210 mL
    The capacity of Pail Y is 3 liters 210 milliliters.

22. $180 \times 5 = 900$
$180 + 900 = 1{,}080$
$1{,}080 \text{ g} = 1{,}000 \text{ g} + 80 \text{ g}$
$\phantom{1{,}080 \text{ g}} = 1 \text{ kg } 80 \text{ g}$
The total mass of Parcel P and Parcel Q is
1 kilogram 80 grams.

23. $5{,}100 - 750 = 4{,}350$
$4{,}350 + 1{,}690 = 6{,}040$
$6{,}040 \text{ m} = 6{,}000 \text{ m} + 40 \text{ m}$
$\phantom{6{,}040 \text{ m}} = 6 \text{ km } 40 \text{ m}$
Road C is 6 kilometers 40 meters long.

24.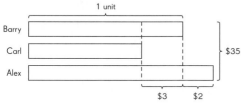

3 units → $\$35 - \$3 - \$3 - \$2 = \$27$
1 unit → $\$27 \div 3 = \$9$
$\$9 + \$3 = \$12$
Barry has \$12.

Chapter 16

Lesson 16.1

1. 11 minutes past 5
   or 49 minutes to 6.

2. 32 minutes past 2
   or 28 minutes to 3.

3. 25 minutes past 6
   or 35 minutes to 7.

4. 39 minutes past 9
   or 21 minutes to 10.

5. 51 minutes past 5
   or 9 minutes to 6.

6. 8:49;
   49 minutes past 8;
   11 minutes to 9
   Accept any 2 answers.

7. 8:21   8. 10:49

9. 18; 7   10. 7; 11

Lesson 16.2

1. 180   2. 105   3. 149   4. 271

5. 378   6. 203   7. 178   8. 282

9. 6   10. 4   11. 5   12. 7

13. 3   14. 1; 35

15. 1; 45   16. 2; 40

17. 3; 15   18. 3; 55

19. 4; 30   20. 5; 5

21. 7; 0

22. 1 h 50 min
    $110 \text{ min} = 60 \text{ min} + 50 \text{ min}$
    $\phantom{110 \text{ min}} = 1 \text{ h} + 50 \text{ min}$
    $\phantom{110 \text{ min}} = 1 \text{ h } 50 \text{ min}$

23. 155 min
    $2 \text{ h } 35 \text{ min} = 60 \text{ min} + 60 \text{ min} + 35 \text{ min}$
    $\phantom{2 \text{ h } 35 \text{ min}} = 155 \text{ min}$

Lesson 16.3

1. 7 h 55 min

   Step 1 $3 \text{ h} + 4 \text{ h} = 7 \text{ h}$

   Step 2 $40 \text{ min} + 15 \text{ min} = 55 \text{ min}$

   Step 3 $7 \text{ h} + 55 \text{ min} = 7 \text{ h } 55 \text{ min}$

2. 8 h 55 min

   Step 1 $2 \text{ h} + 6 \text{ h} = 8 \text{ h}$

   Step 2 $35 \text{ min} + 20 \text{ min} = 55 \text{ min}$

   Step 3 $8 \text{ h} + 55 \text{ min} = 8 \text{ h } 55 \text{ min}$

3. 9 h 35 min

   Step 1 $4 \text{ h} + 5 \text{ h} = 9 \text{ h}$

   Step 2 $5 \text{ min} + 30 \text{ min} = 35 \text{ min}$

   Step 3 $9 \text{ h} + 35 \text{ min} = 9 \text{ h } 35 \text{ min}$

4. a. 6 h 53 min   b. 4 h 50 min
   c. 6 h 53 min   d. 9 h 3 min
   e. 10 h 15 min   f. 11 h 5 min
   g. 12 h 17 min   h. 11 h 5 min
   i. 13 h 30 min

Lesson 16.4

1. 1 h 5 min

   Step 1 $4 \text{ h} - 3 \text{ h} = 1 \text{ h}$

   Step 2 $25 \text{ min} - 20 \text{ min} = 5 \text{ min}$

   Step 3 $1 \text{ h} + 5 \text{ min} = 1 \text{ h } 5 \text{ min}$

2. 5 h 15 min

   Step 1 $8 \text{ h} - 3 \text{ h} = 5 \text{ h}$

   Step 2 $45 \text{ min} - 30 \text{ min} = 15 \text{ min}$

   Step 3 $5 \text{ h} + 15 \text{ min} = 5 \text{ h } 15 \text{ min}$

3. a. 7 h 18 min b. 7 h 44 min
    c. 13 h 37 min d. 6 h 47 min
    e. 14 h 32 min f. 6 h 30 min
    g. 13 h 37 min

Lesson 16.5

1. 10:20 P.M. 2. 1:25 P.M.

3. 2 h 30 min

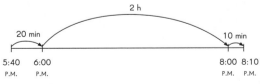

4. 3 h 40 min

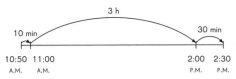

5. Mason started repairing the fence at 1:50 P.M.

    2 hours before 4:25 P.M. is 2:25 P.M.
    35 minutes before 2:25 P.M. is 1:50 P.M.

6. The supermarket closes at 10:00 P.M.

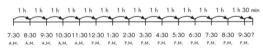

    14 hours after 7:30 P.M. is 9:30 P.M.
    30 minutes after 9:30 P.M. is 10:00 P.M.

7. Their learning journey is 5 hours 45 minutes long.

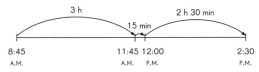

    3 h + 15 min + 2 h 30 min = 5 h 45 min

8. The trip to the library took 2 hours 30 minutes.

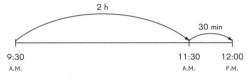

    2 h + 30 min = 2 h 30 min

9. Tom slept for 7 hours 45 minutes.

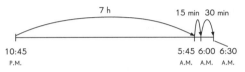

    7 h + 15 min + 30 min = 7 h 45 min

Lesson 16.6

1. 80°F; warm or hot 2. 32°F; cold

3. 105°F; hot 4. 55°F; cool

5. 45°F; cool or cold 6. 85°F; warm or hot

7. 120°F; hot 8. 20°F; cold

9. 69°F, 76°F, 96°F

10. 64°F, 52°F, 46°F

11. People are swimming in a pool.

12. The temperature would be 68°F.

13. 72°F − 50°F = 22°F
    The classroom is 22°F warmer.

14. 212°F 15. 32°F

Lesson 16.7

1. 205 minutes
    3 h 25 min = 60 min + 60 min + 60 min
    + 25 min
    = 205 min

2. It took Karen 2 hours 40 minutes to make the cake.

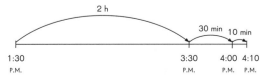

    2 h + 30 min + 10 min = 2 h 40 min

3. Matthew takes 35 minutes to reach school.

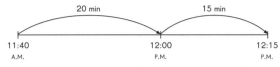

    20 min + 15 min = 35 min

4. The boat ride is 1 hour 25 minutes long.

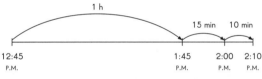

    1 h + 15 min + 10 min = 1 h 25 min

5. Marian practices ballet for 2 hours 15 minutes.
1 h 30 min + 45 min = 1 h 75 min
1 h 75 min = 1 h + 60 min + 15 min
$$\begin{aligned} &= 1\ h + 1\ h + 15\ min \\ &= 2\ h + 15\ min \\ &= 2\ h\ 15\ min \end{aligned}$$

6. Mr. Cruise takes 4 hours 35 minutes altogether.
2 h 40 min + 1 h 55 min
$$\begin{aligned} &= 3\ h\ 95\ min \\ &= 4\ h\ 35\ min \end{aligned}$$

7. Richard takes 6 hours 13 minutes to bake.
2 h 25 min + 3 h 48 min
$$\begin{aligned} &= 5\ h\ 73\ min \\ &= 6\ h\ 13\ min \end{aligned}$$

8. Gary takes 1 hour 15 minutes longer.
2 h 40 min − 1 h 25 min
$$= 1\ h\ 15\ min$$

9. The Saturday practice is 1 hour 15 minutes shorter.
3 h = 2 h 60 min
2 h 60 min − 1 h 45 min
$$= 1\ h\ 15\ min$$

10. Rosie returns home 1 hour 15 minutes earlier.
3 h 10 min = 2 h 70 min
2 h 70 min − 1 h 55 min
$$= 1\ h\ 15\ min$$

11. The difference between temperatures is 28°F.
80°F − 52°F = 28°F

12. It should get 85°F hotter before putting in the pizza.
450°F − 365°F = 85°F

Put on Your Thinking Cap!

1. Thinking skills: Deduction, Sequencing

Strategy: Use a diagram

Solution:
15 min + 18 min + 25 min = 58 min

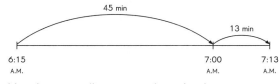

Yes, Joanne will arrive at the school on time at 7:13 A.M.

2. Thinking skills: Deduction, Sequencing

Strategy: Use a diagram

Solution:

1 h 30 min = 90 min
90 min ÷ 5 = 18 min
A plane will leave the airport every 18 minutes.
The third plane will leave at 9:21 A.M.

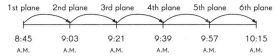

3. Thinking skills: Deduction, Sequencing

Strategy: Use a diagram

Solution:

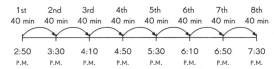

She will apply the ointment for the last time at 7:30 P.M.

4. Thinking skills: Classifying, Deduction

Strategy: Make a systematic list

Solution:

Step 1	Cross out the dates on Saturdays and Sundays: 6 7 13 14 20 21 27 28
Step 2	Cross out the 1-digit dates: 1 2 3 4 5 8 9
Step 3	Cross out the dates which are not multiples of 2: 11 15 17 19 23 25 29 31 Dates left: 10 12 16 18 22 24 26 30
Step 4	1 + 8 = 9

Kayne's birthday is on March 18th.

5. Thinking skill: Deduction

Strategy: Make suppositions

Solution:
There are 31 − 7 = 24 days left in August.
24 + 6 = 30
Marina's birthday is 30 days from today.
30 ÷ 7 = 4 R 2
2 days after Monday is Wednesday.
Marina's birthday is on a Wednesday.

Chapter 17

Lesson 17.1

1. ✓
2. ✓
3. ✗
4. ✓
5. ✓
6. ✗

7. Any two angles.

8. Any two angles.

9. Any two angles.

10. Any two angles.

11. Any two angles.

12. Any two angles.

Encyclopedia

Lesson 17.2

1.

Smaller than a Right Angle	Equal to a Right Angle	Larger than a Right Angle
Angle B Angle F	Angle A Angle C	Angle D Angle E

2. E
3. F

4. H

5. I

6. J

7. T

8.  4

9. 5

Lesson 17.3

1. Segments *AB* and *BC*
   Segments *AE* and *ED*

2. Segments *FG* and *GH*
   Segments *HI* and *IJ*

3. Segments *UP* and *PQ*
   Segments *UT* and *TS*

4. Segments *UV* and *VW*
   Segments *VW* and *WY*

5. Segments *AB* and *BC*
   Segments *DE* and *EF*
   Segments *AF* and *FE*

6. Segments *GH* and *HI*
   Segments *LM* and *MN*
   Segments *MN* and *NO*

7. Segments *QR* and *RS*
   Segments *VP* and *PQ*

Lesson 17.4

1.

2.

3.

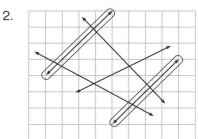

4. Segments *AB* and *DC*
   Segments *BC* and *AD*
5. Segments *EF* and *HG*
6. Segments *PQ* and *TS*
   Segments *QR* and *UT*
   Segments *RS* and *UP*

Put on Your Thinking Cap!

Thinking skill: Spatial visualization

1.

Shape	Number of Sides	Number of Angles	Number of Right Angles
◺	3	3	1
▢	4	4	4
▱	4	4	0
⬠	5	5	0
⬡	6	6	0
⊏⊐	12	12	8

2. Answers vary.
   Sample answer:

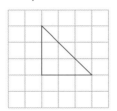

3. Answers vary.
   Sample answer:

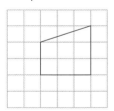

4. Answers vary.
   Sample answer:

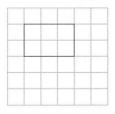

5. Answers vary.
   Sample answer:

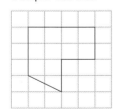

Chapter 18

Lesson 18.1

1. square
2. trapezoid
3. hexagon
4. triangle

---

5. octagon
6. rhombus
7. pentagon
8. rectangle
9. parallelogram

10.

Polygons	Number of Sides	Number of Vertices	Number of Angles
triangle	3	3	3
square	4	4	4
pentagon	5	5	5
hexagon	6	6	6
octagon	8	8	8

11. False
12. False
13. True
14. True
15. True
16. True

17. parallelogram; A parallelogram has 2 pairs of opposite sides that are parallel.
    Only the opposite sides of parallelogram need to be of equal length. There are 4 angles.

18. trapezoid; A trapezoid has 1 pair of opposite sides that are parallel. There are 4 angles. A trapezoid can have 2 right angles.

19. rhombus; Opposite sides of a rhombus are parallel. A rhombus has all sides that are of equal length. There are 4 angles.

20. Answers vary.
    Sample answer: A rhombus has all sides that are of equal length but a parallelogram only has opposite sides that need to be of equal length.

21. Answers vary.
    Sample answer: Both are quadrilaterals and therefore, polygons. Both have at least one pair of opposite sides that is parallel.

22. True	23. True
24. False	25. True
26. True	27. True

Lesson 18.2

1. yes	2. no
3. yes	4. yes
5. yes	6. no
7.	8.

9.

Lesson 18.3

1. Yes	2. yes
3. yes	4. yes

5. yes

6. no
7. yes

8. no	9. yes
10. yes	11. yes
12. no	13. yes
14. no	

Put on Your Thinking Cap!

Thinking skill: Classifying

Strategy: Act it out

Solution: Answers vary.

198   Answers

Chapter 19

Lesson 19.1

1. Answers vary.
   Sample answer:

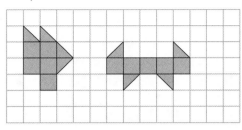

2. 8
3. 10
4. 9
5. 7
6. 11
7. 11

Lesson 19.2

1. 11
2. 10
3. 10
4. 8
5. Answers vary.
   Sample answer:

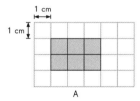

6. Answers vary.
   Sample answer:

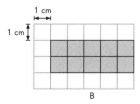

7. B

8. I can add squares or half-squares to figure A to make its area 10 square centimeters or I can remove square or half-squares from Figure B to make its area 6 square centimeters.

9. Answers vary.
   Sample answer:

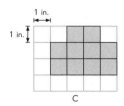

C

10. Answers vary.
    Sample answer:

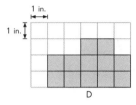

D

11. C

12. I can add squares or half squares to Figure C to make its area 12 square inches or remove squares or half squares from figure D to make its area 10 square inches.

Lesson 19.3

1. 11
2. 16
3. 12
4. 4
5. Answers vary. Sample answer: 2 or 3
6. Answers vary. Sample answer: 2 or 4
7. Answers vary. Sample answer: magazine, paper napkin
8. Answers vary.
9. Answers vary.
10. Answers vary. Sample answer: rug, window

Lesson 19.4

1. Perimeter = 14 cm
   Area = 8 cm^2
2. Perimeter = 12 cm
   Area = 5 cm^2
3. Perimeter = 16 in.
   Area = 8 in.^{2}
4. Perimeter = 24 in.
   Area = 11 in.^{2}
5. Perimeter = 22 m
   Area = 10 m^2

6. Perimeter = 20 m
   Area = 14 m^2
7. Perimeter = 20 ft
   Area = 12 ft^2
8. Perimeter = 22 ft
   Area = 13 ft^2
9. Answer vary.
   Sample answer:

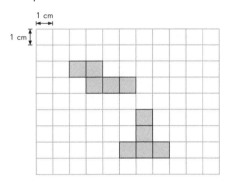

10. Answers vary.

Lesson 19.5

1. Perimeter = 8 cm + 4 cm + 4 cm + 6 cm
   + 12 cm
   = 34 cm
2. Perimeter = 8 cm + 6 cm + 5 cm + 4 cm
   + 4 cm + 6 cm
   = 33 cm
3. Perimeter = 7 in. + 2 in. + 7 in. + 7 in.
   + 2 in. + 7 in. + 7 in.
   = 39 in.
4. Perimeter = 4 in. + 5 in. + 5 in. + 4 in.
   + 6 in. + 6 in.
   = 30 in.
5. 36
6. 30
7. 42
8. Perimeter of a square card = 15 + 15 + 15 + 15
   = 60 cm
   Total length of ribbon used = 60 × 3
   = 180 cm
9. 1 side ⟶ 24 ÷ 8 = 3 m
   Perimeter of each square table
   = 3 + 3 + 3 + 3
   = 12 m

Put on Your Thinking Cap!

1. Thinking skills: Identify patterns and relationships

   Strategy: Look for pattern(s)

   Solution:

Side (cm)	Perimeter (cm)	Area (cm²)
1	4	1
2	8	4
3	12	9
4	16	16
5	20	25

2. 4

3. 25

4. Thinking skills: Spatial visualization, Comparing

   Strategy: Use a diagram

   Solution:

   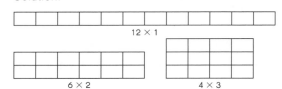

   12×1

   6×2 4×3

5. Thinking skills: Spatial visualization, Comparing

   Strategy: Use a diagram

   Solution: 130 cm

End-of-Year Test Prep

1. A	2. B	3. C	4. C
5. A	6. A	7. B	8. B
9. C	10. D	11. A	12. A
13. B	14. C	15. A	16. D
17. B	18. C	19. A	20. C

21.

22. a. 180, 220

    b. 210

23. 2 kg 800 g

24. 5

25. a. 6

    b. 10

26. $\frac{3}{4}, \frac{2}{3}, \frac{7}{12}$

27. $\frac{1}{3}$

28. Segments BC and CD

29. 346

30. Answers vary.

    Sample answers:

    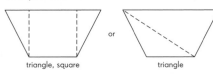

    triangle, square   or   triangle

31. 2 h 40 min

32. 9:35 P.M.

33. 12

34. Segments AF and CD or FE and BC or AB and ED

35. 2 L 100 mL

36. 80

37. 60

38. 280

39. 9

40. 18

41. 1 kg 840 g = 1,000 g + 840 g

    　　　　　　 = 1,840 g

    1,840 − 595 = 1,245

    1,245 g = 1,000 g + 245 g

    　　　　 = 1 kg 245 g

    Box B has a mass of 1 kilogram 245 grams.

42. $50 × 6 = $300

    $300 + $160 = $460

    Grandma Li had $460 at first.

43. 5,060 − 1,680 = 3,380

    The distance between Point B and Point C is 3,380 meters.

    5,060 + 3,380 = 8,440

    8,440 m = 8,000 km + 440 m

    　　　　 = 8 km 440 m

    The distance between Point A and Point C is 8 kilometers 440 meters.

44.

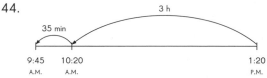

Kate goes to school at 9:45 A.M.

45. 8 quarters = $2

    22 dimes = $2.20

    $2 + $2.20 = $4.20

    Jeron has 8 quarters.